A

Why Johnny Still Can't Read or Write or Understand Math

"Stephen King? A piker: no horror story is as harrowing as Andrew Bernstein's must-read *Why Johnny Still Can't Read or Write or Understand Math*. Bernstein tears the genteel cover off the educational system and reveals the truly shocking extent of the destruction that has been wrought by fashionable Leftist educational theories, the con men, quacks and psychopaths who have gained control of American public education over the last few decades, and the public educational system's addiction to taxpayer funding and the latest societal trends, no matter how damaging they are to children. But Bernstein doesn't just leave us screaming: he also offers a practical, readily applicable program for taking back the educational system and saving our children from these lunatics. If you have children in school, this is essential reading. And even if you don't, but care about the future of society, you must not miss this all-important book."

–Robert Spencer, bestselling author of *The History of Jihad, Did Muhammad Exist?* **and** *The Critical Qur'an*

"Andrew Bernstein eloquently describes the alarming state of American public education today, explores the reasons for its decline, and offers much-needed solutions, emphasizing the crucial role of parents and the importance of school choices and privatization."

–Nora Dimitrova Clinton, PhD, Co-Founder and President, American Research Center in Bulgaria

"With Andrew Bernstein's charming passion, his wealth of knowledge, and his renownedability as a master teacher, he solves the mystery of why American education has deteriorated dramatically. *Who is crippling the minds of our children and how is this happening? Who are the enemies of academic training? What can you, as a parent or educator, do about it?* Dr. Bernstein exposes the perpetrators of the broken American educational system, their motives, their methods, and the causes of their entrenched power. He contrasts them with the heroes and heroines in education such as Maria Montessori and Marva Collins. He shows parents, teachers, and anyone wanting children to develop a *love* of learning, how to "outflank" the educational establishment. *What would foster a deep love of learning?* This fascinating page-turner offers parents creative solutions and a glimpse into a proper education. With solid academic training, our children would finish their school years with a depth of knowledge in the key academic fields, giving them confidence in their own minds, and the independent thinking skills to pursue happiness in their own lives. Further, it would repair the crippling harm done to the self-esteem of thousands of semi-illiterate victims of our school system, heartbreaking harm that I haveseen in my professional work."

–Ellen Kenner, Ph.D., Clinical Psychologist

"Andrew Bernstein begins his book with an exposéof the current educational crisis and how we got there. He shows that the teachers colleges, the state and federal departments of education, and local administrators form an impenetrable fortress imposing on the schools mind-destroying educational policies. He goes on to offer solutions such as homeschooling, micro schools, small community schools and other private schools, various forms of tutoring, and ultimately, the privatization of government schools. It is in our rational self-interest to study *Why Johnny Can't Read or Write or Understand Math* and advocate for the changes suggested."

–Edwin Thompson, Founder, Conceptual Education Fellowship
https://aynrand.org/educators/conceptual-education-fellowship/

"Andrew Bernstein has given us a ground-breaking tour-de-force on how the American educational system has destroyed the mind and spirit of American youth. Rich in historical detail, Bernstein traces the antecedents of the war against the human mind and the motives behind the architects of progressive education. Every American with a child should read this book. Every person interested in understanding how unchallenged idea pathogens can still contaminate even the best of minds must read this book. Bernstein provides solutions to the problems identified. In so doing, even the adult mind is inoculated against a culture bent on enshrining mediocrity and destroying greatness. This book is a work of moral heroism."

–Jason D. Hill

"Andrew Bernstein has written a book for our time. No topic in American cultural life is hotter right now than education, andWhy Johnny Still Can't Read or Write or Understand Mathis going to shake-up how Americans see the government schoolsystem. With an avalanche of evidence, witheringlogic, powerful analysis, and crystal clear prose, Bernstein smashes the argument for Progressive education and government schooling with a philosophic hammer.If you love your children, you must read this book. If you read this book, you must pull your kids from America's government schools. It'sthat simple. #JustWalkAway."

–C. Bradley Thompson, author, *America's Revolutionary Mind*

"In his newest book, Dr. Andrew Bernstein leads us along a clear path to understanding one of the greatest tragedies that has been unfolding within our culture. *Why Johnny Still Can't Read or Write or Understand Math* is a straight-forward, objective review of current American education, including its historical roots, the shifts in ideas that influenced the purpose, content and methods of teaching, and the resulting horrific impact on American children. Then, he gives us hope. Bernstein provides brutally honest evaluations of where parents are stonewalled and unlikely to affect systemic change in the public schools. But he also identifies a variety of small and larger efforts parents can make to help their children gain the knowledge and skills they need to become independent thinkers who can live well and flourish. This book provides sound practical advice that any parent can adopt to substantially improve his/her child's education. This book is a must read for anyone sincerely concerned to improve education in this country."

–Lori Rice, Ph.D., Behavioral Scientist

Why Johnny Still Can't Read

or Write

or Understand Math

And What We Can Do About It

Andrew Bernstein

BOMBARDIER
B O O K S

Published by Bombardier Books
An Imprint of Post Hill Press
ISBN: 978-1-63758-433-0
ISBN (eBook): 978-1-63758-434-7

Why Johnny Still Can't Read or Write or Understand Math:
And What We Can Do About It
© 2022 by Andrew Bernstein
All Rights Reserved

Cover Design by Tiffani Shea
Interior Design by Yoni Limor

BOMBARDIER
BOOKS

PRESS

Post Hill Press
New York • Nashville
posthillpress.com

Published in the United States of America
1 2 3 4 5 6 7 8 9 10

*"Our greatest natural resource is the
minds of our children."*

—Walt Disney

*"The doors of the world are opened to
people who can read."*

—Ben Carson, M.D.

To Penelope Joy,
My gem of a daughter

Contents

PART TWO
How We Can Fix the Educational Disaster

Introduction

Let's start with true stories. A few years ago, a college student in my philosophy course wrote "looshly" several times in a paper. I thought, "Looshly? What is that?" After coming across this word three or four times, I finally realized from the contexts that she meant "usually." A student in college thought that "usually" was spelled "looshly." (That is a very "loosh" spelling indeed.) This is one vivid example of the spelling ability of many of today's college students.

Just recently, I had occasion to note another. On a midterm exam, a student spelled a particular word as "speortat." Again, I wondered, "What word is that?" The second time he used it on the exam, the context told me he meant "separate." There are many more such incidents I could share because, unfortunately, true stories like these are common.

One more: In a college logic course last year, I used James Madison as an example. There were twenty students in the class, all of them born, reared, and educated in the United States, so it seemed a safe bet that they knew who he was. Not so safe, as it turned out. Ten of the students had never heard of him. Ten had heard of him as a former president of the United States. Not one of the twenty knew that he was the lead author of the US Constitution or that he was virtually the sole author of the Bill of Rights.

Unfortunately, these occurrences in college classrooms are now common. This horrifying level of ignorance among high school graduates is becoming the norm. How do we fix it? How do we raise US schooling to a much higher level? There are several things that must be done. But first and foremost is this:

> *Parents must have full control over the education of their children.*

This book will return to that theme over and over again. Teachers, tutors, and schools can advise—but parents must have the final authority regarding the content and methods of their children's education.

This book is intended for a popular audience, especially parents, and so there are no endnotes. Readers who seek documentation can find it in the books listed in the Bibliography at the end of this book. Parents need to know the shocking truth that our kids aren't failing in school—rather, the schools are failing our kids. Above all, they need to know how we can fix the terrible mess that our school system has become.

This book was inspired by Rudolf Flesch's famous 1955 book, *Why Johnny Can't Read*. Flesch, an Austrian immigrant to the United States, pointed out that there were no remedial reading problems in European nations because their educational systems employed systematic phonics to teach children to read. This means they taught young children the alphabet, and taught them the various sounds made when those letters and combinations of letters are spoken aloud. Similarly, Flesch pointed out that prior to roughly the 1920s, there were few or no reading problems in the United States either...for the same reason. Reading problems began and multiplied after that in this country because the schools started to phase out the use of phonics in favor of the "whole-word" method. With this method, students are not taught to sound out a word's letters; in many cases they are not even allowed to. Rather, they are expected to look at the shape of a word and guess what it is from its context. So, for example, for the sentence "I like to eat carrots," a student who reads it as "I like to eat cake" is praised for making a good guess. "Cake" and "carrots" have a roughly similar shape, and either makes sense in the context of the sentence. There are tens of thousands of words in the English language; indeed, several major dictionaries include some 470,000 entries; so it is impossible to memorize the shape of each. Therefore, our kids are taught to guess—and praised for making a guess that, within a given context, is plausible. Martin Gross, in his book, *The Conspiracy of Ignorance*, quoted advocates of this method who claimed that reading is "a psycholinguistic guessing game."

Except that it isn't. Flesch pointed out that the abandonment of phonics in favor of the whole-word method was the reason that so many Americans struggled to read. He was right. Today, it is still the reason.

The problem, in many cases, is not with the teachers. There are still many excellent classroom teachers in the public school system, as well as in many private schools.

This book is written for them as well—and for millions of grandparents, other relatives of schoolchildren, and close friends of their families. Finally, the book is directed to millions of solid citizens across the republic that, regardless of their political affiliation or religious beliefs, recognize that American students need and deserve a better education than they currently receive, and that the kids' futures and the future of the country we love depend on it.

This book is not written specifically for college professors or other professional intellectuals—although they can certainly benefit from it. College professors, after all—including myself—inherit students who in many cases have been academically crippled by our failed school system.

Most Americans know something is horribly wrong with the US education system. For example, they hear on a regular basis how poorly American kids score on various standardized tests, including international ones. In this case, what they know anecdotally is backed by facts. The American education system in general is very bad, has been so for a long time, and is getting steadily worse.

Let's look at the results of the 2019 National Assessment of Educational Progress (NAEP) tests, which are sometimes referred to as the nation's "report card." These tests are given to some six hundred thousand fourth- and eighth-grade students in all fifty states. The results were dismal, especially in the all-important area of reading. In seventeen states, fourth-grade reading scores—already starting from a low baseline—not only showed no progress but actually *dropped even lower* than the 2017 results. The eighth graders performed even worse: Their reading scores on average dropped in thirty-one states. Further, the eighth graders scored a point lower on average in math compared with 2017. In math, fourth graders were the only group to show any improvement—and by only one point, going on average from 240 to 241 *out of a possible 500*. I was never the world's greatest math student—going to the public schools did not help that—but even I can figure out that 241 out of 500 is below 50 percent...not very good. Further, Project Baltimore points out that in 2022 at one Baltimore high school, fewer than two percent of the 628 students read at grade level; out of 484 students, 77 percent, read at an elementary school level, including 71 who were reading at a kindergarten level and eighty-eight reading at a first-grade level.

Internationally, the results are also bad. For example, the Program for International Student Assessment (PISA) is a worldwide study that every three years tests fifteen-year-olds on their knowledge of reading, math, and science. It tests some 540,000 students in seventy-two countries. In 2015, the US kids did not crack the top ten nations in any of the three fields; in fact, they did not crack the top twenty. They ranked thirty-fifth in math, twenty-fifth in science, and twenty-fourth in reading. American students' average math scores dropped eleven points in 2015 compared with 2012—and remained flat in reading and science. More recently, the 2018 PISA results showed a lack of progress. American kids remained below the international average in math and, among the seventy-nine nations that participated, remained average in reading. These results are similar to the 2019 NAEP scores—each of these tests show American stagnation. (The 2021 PISA test was postponed due to COVID-19 restrictions.) Despite all the attention and money lavished on the US school system, it has made little or no progress. *The school system of the wealthiest and most powerful nation in history has no idea how to improve its poor educational performance.*

I went to the public schools in Brooklyn, New York, in the 1960s. My whole early schooling, K–12, was in the public schools. Looking back now, I realize that the schools were not good then. They have gotten much worse during the more than forty years I've been teaching at New York–area colleges. I and many of my friends who also are college professors have seen the decline firsthand.

We all report the same heartbreaking truths. At "good" colleges, many students struggle just to read effectively and certainly cannot read at a college level. I hold a PhD in philosophy, and that is the subject I teach. I would like my students to read primary sources—works by thinkers such as Plato, Aristotle, John Locke, David Hume, and so forth. But many of them cannot do it. Struggling with the basic mechanics of reading, as many do, they cannot comprehend the difficult material.

Additionally, again and again I have seen—and my colleagues report—that the overwhelming number of today's college students cannot write college-level essays. In many cases, they do not even come close. In too many cases, they cannot write a grammatical paragraph. And their spelling is often atrocious. We have already seen two examples of this as well as an example of the generally poor state of students' knowledge of history.

Recently, I witnessed another example of this ignorance of history. Only one student out of twenty-five in my Introduction to Philosophy course knew that the First Amendment to the US Constitution contains the "Establishment" clause, certifying that there will not be a state-established, government-mandated religion in this country that the citizens are required to practice, and that freedom of religion will be upheld. My initial emotional response was elation. Then I thought, "One out of twenty-five? I'm happy with that? Have we really lowered the bar that much?" It's not good to normalize ignorance as a natural state among American citizens. The ignorance among today's college students regarding our own country's history would be shocking if I hadn't learned to expect it.

One final example: My daughter is truly a great kid. She is honest, hardworking, responsible, and as good-hearted as any human being can be. I am very proud of her. As I write this, she is a twelfth grader in what is considered to be a very good suburban public high school. What do you think she and her classmates are reading in their twelfth-grade English courses?

Let me provide a little background first. I was such a troublemaker in school that I was kicked out of all the advanced placement, honors, and honors background English courses that the public high schools offered back in the 1960s. So I was in a garden-variety twelfth-grade English course in a public high school in Brooklyn. We read a number of books, and the two I remember are Shakespeare's *Macbeth* and Dostoyevsky's *Crime and Punishment*. Of course, we wrote essays about each book, which the teacher corrected. Then the teacher would work with us on our understanding and our writing.

Further, in the 1980s, when I was in graduate school, I taught eleventh-grade English, twelfth- grade English, and twelfth-grade philosophy in a small, private school in White Plains, New York. We had some very good students, and, as in any school, some not so good. But we held them to high educational standards, we had strong expectations for the students, and we pushed them. In my twelfth-grade English course, my students read Sophocles' *Oedipus the King*, Euripides' *Medea*, excerpts from the Bible, Shakespeare's *Hamlet* and *King Lear*, Victor Hugo's *Les Misérables*, Dostoyevsky's *The Brothers Karamazov*, and Ayn Rand's *Atlas Shrugged*. Of course, the students wrote detailed essays on each of these works, and I worked with them on their writing.

Back to my daughter and her classmates. What are twelfth-grade English students at an "excellent" suburban public high school reading today? Are they reading Shakespeare and Dostoyevsky? They are not. Are they studying other great literary classics? They are not. Are they reading other novels, plays, and short stories that, although perhaps not classics, are still well-written and deal with timeless human themes? They are not. What are they reading? Nothing. They are reading nothing. Class time is spent, rather, helping the students write their college essays.

Now, at least this helps the kids improve their writing… and has a practical benefit. *But an entire high school year goes by without enhancing the students' knowledge of, and appreciation for, the world's great literature.* What a waste! It is disgraceful. No wonder that the famous scholar Richard Pipes stated that applicants for his freshman course at

Harvard were almost totally unfamiliar with the world's great literature. *At Harvard!*

Rather than working on college essays in twelfth-grade English class, the teachers should be discussing great novels and dramas seriously. They should have the students write essays on these great works. Then they should correct the essays and show the kids how to improve both their understanding and their writing. *Further, teachers should have been doing this consistently from first grade onward* (starting with such excellent children's books as *Peter Pan*, *The Secret Garden*, *Anne of Green Gables*, and so forth, and building steadily to more advanced books). It is unreasonable to expect students in the early elementary grades to write essays, but they can write brief paragraphs and, gradually, build toward essays. If all this were to happen, how much help would twelfth-grade English students even need in writing their college essays?

And what about the kids who do not intend to attend college but who plan to do something else with their lives? Doesn't their education require all the more that they learn about great literature in twelfth grade?

Since I teach philosophy, I have lots of opportunities to see the kids' lack of knowledge in history and literature and their struggles with reading, writing, and spelling. There is not much opportunity to discuss math or science, but I understand from colleagues in those fields that the situation is much the same. Why wouldn't it be? If the schools largely do not teach the kids reading, writing, literature, or history, why would we expect them to teach students math or science?

This book aims to do four things. First, it will show, based on facts, that the US education system is in big trouble. Second, it will show that prior to the early twentieth century, it was generally outstanding—and can be again. Third, it will demonstrate how the collapse of the American education system occurred, who caused it to occur, and why those people did so. This book will point fingers. It will name names, and it will be specific. Fourth, above all, it will show what we can do to greatly improve the education that our children receive.

If you want to skip the first half of the book and go right to the chapters on what we can do to improve schooling, you can certainly do so. But remember: We are much better able to cure a disease when we know the germs that cause it.

I want to reiterate that there are still many good classroom teachers in every grade of the public school system and in the private schools as well. They are not the problem. The early sections of this book discuss where the problems have come from, who caused them, and why. But for now, we should remember that there are many outstanding classroom teachers who, in order to do a great job for their students, must fight against a stifling bureaucracy and who get burned out, retire young, and/or move into different careers. Through no fault of the students, schoolkids are thereby deprived of many of our best teachers.

Marva Collins is a perfect example of this. She had no teaching degree but taught in the Chicago public schools in the 1960s because of a teacher shortage. Not having gone through the horrors of a college education program, she was more independent in her thinking, more willing to scorn the failed policies of the government bureaucracies, and better equipped to follow her own judgment regarding the best methods of teaching. She rejected the Department of Education's favored (and unsuccessful) whole-word method of teaching reading and employed phonics instead. She introduced great works of literature and poetry into her classes, had the students analyze these works in depth, and based her disciplinary methods on positive rewards rather than on punishment. Not surprisingly, her methods were highly effective.

But more than a decade of battling against bureaucratic mentalities intent on enforcing the state's mind-numbing curriculum weighed heavily on her. In the mid-1970s, she resigned from the public schools and taught a handful of elementary students in the basement of a local college. Eventually, on the second floor of her own home, she founded her own academy; it started as a tiny one-room school and grew eventually into Chicago's famed Westside Preparatory School—at which, for decades, its students achieved outstanding academic results. Many of her students were from poor families and/or were minorities that the public schools did not think capable of gaining a superb education. But Marva Collins cultivated outstanding reading abilities in her students by drilling them constantly with the phonetic method; she even used phonics when teaching math. Her students, over and over again, became such accomplished readers that they enjoyed reading (and understanding) Shakespeare and other classics by the third grade.

This is what is possible in the field of education. But repeatedly, outstanding teachers like Marva Collins are frustrated by the antieducational policies of our public schools and leave those schools for better opportunities. Because almost 90 percent of American students ages five to seventeen go to the public schools, the overwhelming bulk of them are thereby denied access to many of the country's top educators, who move to private schools or out of the field altogether.

This is but the tip of the iceberg of our education system's failings. So let me leave you with some shocking but true claims that will move us into the worst of the school system's problems. Do you know why many American students struggle to read? Because the schools that teach our teachers do not want them to read.

Similarly, do you know why American students know so little about academic subjects? Because the schools that teach our teachers do not want them to learn academic subjects.

Don't believe me? Keep reading to find out the truth.

PART ONE

The Current Crisis of American
Schooling and How It Happened

CHAPTER ONE

The Terrible State of American Schooling

In May 2021, a story broke that 109 teachers and administrators in Atlanta were being investigated for possible cheating on standardized tests. There were suspicions about gains made by students, and investigations showed an unusual number of erasures on the tests. Investigators were seeking to determine if teachers and administrators were responsible for the unexpectedly high scores. Recently, there was also a school cheating scandal in the Houston area that resulted in the resignation of the principal, the assistant principal, and three teachers. Further, investigations in Massachusetts, Indiana, Virginia, and Nevada also point to cheating by teachers on standardized tests.

This is what it's come to in American schooling. The students' test scores are so weak that teachers and administrators feel compelled to cheat in order to make the school system look better.

Almost every day, we hear horror stories about the public school system, so I won't go on and on with these tales of woe. A handful will be plenty to show the sorry state of current US schooling, and the many years of decline that led to it. We need to realize that *this educational horror has been going on for a long time.*

As far back as the 1980s, President Ronald Reagan's secretary of education appointed a commission to study the sorry state of American schooling. In 1983, the commission published its report. It was titled "A Nation at Risk" and concluded ominously: "If an unfriendly foreign power had attempted to impose on America the mediocre educational performance that exists today, we might well have viewed it as an act of war. As it stands, we have allowed this to happen to ourselves."

We have done more than allow it to happen. We have caused it. And we continue to cause it.

We've already discussed how poorly students did in math and reading on the NAEP tests in 2019. But abysmal scores on NAEP tests are nothing new. In 1986, the NAEP administered a test to nearly eight thousand eleventh-grade students nationwide to determine their knowledge of history and literature. It consisted of 262 questions in these two fields, measuring basic knowledge that literate persons should have—that is, things that high school juniors should know if they have had anything resembling a decent education.

The results? The average score in history (mostly American history) was 54.5 percent. In literature, the results were even worse: The average score was 51.8 percent. In both cases, the average scores were not even close to passing grades.

In the history portion, 31.9 percent of the students did not know that Columbus reached the New World before 1750. (Whatever happened to "In fourteen hundred and ninety-two, Columbus sailed the ocean blue"?) I can keep citing these awful numbers, but I suspect there is no reason to overwhelm you with statistics. So I will simplify and say that a large number of the kids did not know that the US Constitution was written between 1750 and 1800, and many also did not know that Japan's attack on Pearl Harbor occurred between 1939 and 1943.

But the really jaw-dropping numbers surround Lincoln's presidency and the US Civil War. Fewer than one student in four knew that Lincoln was president between 1860 and 1880. A substantial subset of the students also selected three other twenty-year periods for Lincoln's presidency: 1800 to 1820, 1820 to 1840, and 1840 to 1860. The sad truth is that roughly as many American eleventh graders thought that Lincoln was president between 1800 and 1820 as realized that he was elected to the nation's highest office only decades later. But perhaps most astonishing is that substantially more than half of the students did not know that the US Civil War occurred between 1850 and 1900; many thought it was fought between 1800 and 1850, and a significant percent believed it took place between1750 and 1800—during most of which time, in fact, the United States as a nation did not even exist.

The literature scores were even worse and reflect, in part, the school's failed method of trying to teach reading. Let's look at only one aspect of the literature test: linking great authors to their most famous works. Only a small number of the kids could identify Dostoyevsky as the author of either of his great novels, *Crime and Punishment* or *The Brothers Karamazov*. All three of the other alternatives offered on this multiple choice question—Anton Chekhov, Boris Pasternak, and Alexander Solzhenitsyn—were chosen more often. A question on the great Norwegian playwright Henrik Ibsen led to similar results. Although three of his greatest works were listed—*Hedda Gabler*, *A Doll's House*, and *An Enemy of the People*—only a small percentage of the students knew that Ibsen wrote any of them.

Making matters worse, students left many of the 262 test questions blank because they didn't know the answers. *But they were marked wrong only for the questions they answered incorrectly*. So their actual scores were even worse than the reported ones.

Two years later, in 1988, a mere 5 percent of seventeen-year-old high school students could read well enough to understand information provided in historic documents, literary essays, or college textbooks. In 1994, the Educational Testing Service (ETS) reported the heartbreaking truths that 50 percent of college graduates in the United States could not read a bus schedule and that only 42 percent could accurately summarize a newspaper article.

Andrew Coulson, in his book, *Market Education*, discussed results from NAEP tests in the 1990s. The 1991 test showed that fewer than half of twelfth graders could do seventh grade work in math; the 1999 test revealed that merely 14 percent of eighth graders understood math at a seventh grade level or above. By 2000, math students in the United States ranked below those in Malaysia, Bulgaria, and Latvia.

More recently, one in three fourth graders scored below the "basic level"—the lowest ranking deemed effective—

in reading on the NAEP tests. Dan Lips, in a 2008 essay titled, "Still a Nation at Risk," published by the Heritage Foundation, pointed out that among low-income students, half score below that level—and in some of America's larger cities, only half the students earn a high school diploma; in Detroit, only one-quarter do. Further, according to literacy statistics published at the website Thinkimpact, "on average, 66 percent of fourth-grade children in the United States could not read proficiently in 2013," and, in 2022, some 21 percent of American adults are illiterate and 54 percent of adults have a literacy level below the sixth grade.

Is it possible that the problems lie primarily with the kids and their families? There is some truth to that. Anyone who has even a little teaching experience knows that many of the students are not motivated to do the work that getting an education requires. And it is definitely true that parents, although busy with work and other responsibilities, should be more involved in their children's education than many currently are. A great deal of research (for example, from the Responsive Classroom website) shows that the best schools—public as well as private—are the ones in which parents are deeply involved. At the best schools, there tends to be a strong Parent Teacher Association (PTA), and parents often help their kids with homework and use phonics to teach their preschoolers reading.

While it is understandable that many parents are tired after working and making sure their children are well-fed and well-clothed, it is still their responsibility to make sure their kids receive both a strong moral training and an effective education. Too many people seem to believe that we drop off our kids at school and take them home afterward, and in the time in between, the schools are educating them. In far too many cases, this belief is false.

Yes, on average, parents need to be more involved. Later in this book, you'll read a great deal about potential good news: parent power. Parents can do a great deal to turn this sorry mess around and make sure their kids get a much better education than they currently do.

But there is no escaping the ugly truth that the prime cause of today's educational disaster is the schools—and the forces that lie behind them. I will raise the following questions: Is it possible to fix the school system? Is it possible to change the forces behind the school system that are responsible for its atrocious performance? Those forces are: 1. teachers' colleges, 2. the state Departments of Education, and 3. the federal Department of Education.

What if, upon examination, we find that we can neither fix the school system nor change the forces that make it so bad? In that case, we will discuss how we can outflank those forces, how we can get around them, and how we can do things *outside of the schools* that will greatly improve the education our kids receive.

Before we explore the reasons that our schools are so bad, who is responsible, and why those people did it, let's remember that it is very encouraging to realize that American education at one time was outstanding. We will look at the superb education provided in this country's earlier days and how this was accomplished. This will provide valuable clues for how we can achieve it again in our day.

CHAPTER TWO

Superb Education in America's Past

Robert Peterson, in an essay titled, "Education in Colonial America," quoted the Reverend Jacob Duché, the first chaplain of Congress. Duché said of everyday Americans in the 1770s, "The poorest laborer upon the shore of the Delaware thinks himself entitled to deliver his sentiments in matters of religion or politics with as much freedom as the gentleman or scholar…. Such is the prevailing taste for books of every kind, that almost every man is a reader."

Wow, imagine this. I'm a philosophy professor, and I've written a number of books. I am also just a kid from Brooklyn, but in the 1770s and 1780s, I could have sat with laborers on the Delaware River docks and conducted fascinating discussions about Thomas Paine's book *Common Sense*, about Thomas Jefferson's wording in the Declaration of Independence, about the essays of *The Federalist*, written by Alexander Hamilton, James Madison, and John Jay as newspaper editorials in support of the new Constitution, and about much else of interest.

"Almost every man is a reader," Duché said. What a contrast with today, when millions of American citizens are functionally illiterate! Let's take a deeper look at American education in the past. It might both instruct us and inspire us to make improvements in the present.

Let's start, for example, in the Middle Atlantic colonies during the pre-Revolutionary period, when professional educators set up many schools to satisfy the demand for education. Philadelphia, for instance, boasted schools for every subject and interest. Between 1740 and 1776, 125 private schoolmasters advertised their services in Philadelphia newspapers—this, in a city whose population was tiny relative to today. Professional educators provided mentoring services in English, contemporary foreign languages, science, and a wide variety of other topics. Children who grew to be brilliant scientists, writers, and statesmen, such as Benjamin Franklin, Thomas Jefferson, and George Washington, received their education at home or in private schools.

The literacy levels of Revolutionary America were very high. In 1731, Franklin helped start America's first subscription library, and similar libraries spread throughout the colonies during his life. Franklin later wrote in his autobiography, "These libraries have improved the general conversation of the Americans, [and] made the common tradesmen and farmers as intelligent as most gentlemen from other countries." Tradesmen and farmers? Were they reading by candlelight after working all day in the stores and the fields? If so, it shows a strong motivation to read on the part of everyday Americans.

Along these same lines, Thomas Paine's pamphlet *Common Sense*, written in plain style but presenting high-level political principles, sold 120,000 copies during the Revolutionary period to a free population of 2.4 million (akin to selling ten million copies today). The essays of *The Federalist* present complex arguments in political philosophy that are, I am unhappy to report, beyond the ability of many American college students today to read or understand. They were largely newspaper editorials written for and read by Everyman.

Noah Webster, who years later became famous for publishing the first dictionary of American English, wrote his *Blue-Backed Speller* in 1783. Webster, a former soldier in the War of Independence, wanted to free the new country from Britain, and from Europe generally, not just in politics but also in language and culture. His spelling book, for example, dropped the letter "k" from the end of such words as "musick." The new American spelling would be "music." So, in many cases, he made spelling less complicated and more straightforward. The *Blue-Backed Speller* sold over one hundred million copies, and for many decades it was used to teach language to American schoolchildren.

Reading and writing were widely taught in the home by parents. There were no public schools in this country back then—there were few or none until the 1850s—and literacy generally was required for admission into private schools. Peterson, speaking again of education in this period, wrote: "Children were often taught to read at home before they were subjected to the rigors of school. In middle-class families, where the mother would be expected to be literate, this was considered part of her duties."

French visitor Pierre Samuel du Pont de Nemours wrote about the high American educational levels near the turn of the nineteenth century. In his book, *National Education in the*

United States of America—commissioned by Vice President Thomas Jefferson—the Frenchman writes: "The United States are more advanced in their educational facilities than most countries. They have a large number of primary schools…. Most young Americans, therefore, can read, write, and cipher [do basic arithmetic]. Not more than four in a thousand are unable to write legibly; while in Spain, Portugal, Italy, only a sixth of the population can read; in Germany, even in France, not more than a third; in Poland, about two men in a hundred; and in Russia not one in two hundred."

He went on to say that in America, most people read the Bible and everyone read newspapers, that the father often read to the children at the breakfast table, and that this practice continued until one of the children read well enough to replace him as primary reader to the family.

Du Pont de Nemours was not the only French visitor to write of the high educational levels in early America. In the 1830s, Alexis de Tocqueville toured the United States. In his famous book *Democracy in America*, he noted about US education that there were only a few scholars who were deeply learned. But he was struck by the high literacy levels of the so-called common man. He wrote of how American pioneers penetrated the backwoods "with the Bible, an axe, and a file of newspapers." He concluded: "[I]f he [a visitor] counts the ignorant, the American people will appear to be the most enlightened community in the world."

Sales of books and educational materials in the early and mid-nineteenth century likewise indicate a high national literacy level. Between 1818 and 1823, when the US population was fewer than twenty million, Walter Scott's novels sold five million copies (the equivalent of selling sixty million copies today). In the early nineteenth century, *The Last of the Mohicans*, by James Fenimore Cooper, likewise sold millions of copies. These books are not easy reading.

The McGuffey's Readers, first published in 1836, were the main primers used to teach reading to American children for the better part of a century. They routinely used such terms as "heath" and "benighted" in third-grade texts. They asked questions such as, "What is this species of composition called?" and gave assignments such as "Relate the facts of this dialogue." The fourth-grade reader included selections from Nathaniel Hawthorne; the fifth-grade text, readings from William Shakespeare. "These were not the textbooks of the elite but of the masses," explains the scholar Thomas Sowell in his book, *Inside American Education*. "From 1836 to 1920, McGuffey's Readers were so widely used that they sold 122 million copies."

We cannot doubt that American education in the past was very good—much better than it is today. But why? Here are the answers.

Earlier, I mentioned Rudolf Flesch and his excellent book *Why Johnny Can't Read*. It was published in 1955, but its main two-part lesson is still relevant today: 1. Throughout American history, until roughly the time of World War I, American parents and schools used phonics to teach reading. Reading levels, as a result, were high and there were few or no cases of remedial reading. 2. In the twentieth century, American educators rejected phonics, preferring something called "look-say," which is a version of the whole-word method. I will have much more to say about the whole-word method and its failings in coming chapters. For now, the point is that educators no longer taught children to sound out the words on the written page; in many cases, they did not even let children do so.

The other reason that American education was so much better in the past is that back then, parents and educators generally understood that the main purpose of education is to train the mind; that is, to teach students to read, to write, to understand math, and to learn history, literature, and science—to put it simply, to teach us how to think and to provide information in important academic fields. In the past, American educators embraced this purpose. To this day, educators in other countries still do. But modern American educators generally do not.

You want to know why American students do so poorly on international tests relative to kids from other countries? You want to know why kids from other countries know so much more about math, history, science, and literature than American kids do? It's because schools in other countries teach these academic subjects much more widely and deeply.

How did this happen? Who made it happen and why? The hair-raising answer is: American educators themselves. The rot begins with John Dewey and his progressive colleagues around the time of World War I. It continues to this day.

Let's go back and understand the process by which they killed the mind of American schools. We will then be better prepared to fix the problems.

CHAPTER THREE
The American War on Reading and Learning Begins

In the early twentieth century, Lewis Terman, a professor at Stanford University, developed an IQ (intelligence quotient) test, often known as the Stanford-Binet test. In the brutal terms of the day, the test was designed to distinguish the gifted kids from the "feeble-minded" ones. Terman and many others who wanted IQ testing in the schools were supporters of eugenics. This was a pseudoscience that was popular one hundred years ago. It claimed that society could be improved by encouraging the "gifted" people to reproduce more widely—and by discouraging the "feeble-minded" from reproducing, even sterilizing them. But in a free country, there was no possibility of legally preventing the latter from reproducing, much less sterilizing them. So what could be done instead? Well, let's see the alternative plan worked out by Terman and the eugenicists.

So-called progressive education is the key. In America the ideas of John Dewey and other progressive "educators" came to dominate the schools of education. The main idea of progressive education is that the schools must teach children

to adjust to society—if necessary, to conform to the group—
and this purpose is more important than teaching them the
academic program—that is, math, literature, history, and
science. Leading progressive educators disagreed on many
points but agreed that a "narrow focus" on academic training
must give way to a program that focused on training the
"whole child."

If this sounds vague, the progressives went on to make
their point more clearly. For example, famed social worker
Jane Addams (1860–1935) was an early progressive reformer
who grumbled that the schools of her day placed too great
an emphasis on reading and writing! She complained that
there was too much "book learning" in the schools, and
claimed that children could be better taught using other
methods. For one thing, she wanted kids to be trained to
work in the factories that were booming in the early days
of the American Industrial Revolution. What she meant,
in particular, was that American kids should be trained to
work collectively in a spirit of teamwork. The progressives
and their modern heirs returned to this emphasis on group
work again and again, in contrast to more individualist,
independent ways of learning, such as sitting alone, reading
a book, and thinking about it.

Progressive educators started to call themselves "educationists," so we can use this terminology to distinguish
them from the professional educators who still believe in
the academic program. The educationists claimed to have a
scientific basis for their preferences in schooling. One such
basis was Terman's IQ test.

As mentioned, Terman hoped that the IQ test would
enable schools to separate out the "feeble-minded" from

the "gifted." The schools could then place these kids on different educational "tracks"—that is, they could give the smart kids the full academic program, and the not-so-smart kids a severely watered-down (or dumbed-down) education. Both groups would be presented differing curricula, with more or much less emphasis on academic subjects. The smarter kids would be guided to college, and the less smart ones would not be; the smart ones would be guided toward careers requiring strong brainpower, and the less smart ones would be guided to careers that involved more manual labor; the smart ones would be groomed to be society's future leaders, and the less smart ones would be groomed to be good workers who loyally followed what society's brainy and educated leaders told them.

In a free country, the "feeble-minded" cannot be prevented from reproducing, so the next best thing was tracking students in the schools. This made sure that the gifted students received a full academic education, and that the less-gifted received mostly vocational training. It also made sure that the less intelligent people had a place in society, a subordinate place as factory and farm workers in which they would obey their more intelligent leaders.

By the 1920s, psychologists had developed dozens of IQ tests to measure the intellectual ability of students of all ages. Millions of students were tested each year. The schools then used this information to decide which kids should be placed on the college track and which would be placed in vocational programs. In practice, of course, this process became a self-fulfilling prophecy, because only the kids on the college track received an education that prepared them for higher learning.

To progressive educators, the IQ tests gave an appearance of science to those reformers who wanted to push millions of kids away from academic education and into vocational training. After all, they believed, American factories were booming and needed workers. American agriculture was growing a large amount of food and needed farmers. The US military was strong enough to make the world safe for democracy and needed soldiers. Of what use were Shakespeare's dramas, Greek or Roman history, mastery of chemistry, or knowledge of calculus to factory workers, plumbers, gardeners, carpenters, farmers, or soldiers? Of little or no use, said the progressives. Rather, these persons needed the skills proper to their profession—vocational training.

The Curriculum Designers

Related to this, again around the time of World War I, several progressives developed the field known as "curriculum studies." John Franklin Bobbitt, a professor at the University of Chicago (and others at various US colleges) held that curriculum design was a complicated field that could be understood only by those who knew the new "scientific" methods of education—that is, IQ testing and the tracking that could be based on it.

Prior to World War I, the schools' curricula had been designed by community school boards, who knew the parents and their expectations. At the time, Americans in almost all towns and neighborhoods desired their children to receive a full academic education—to learn reading, writing, spelling, grammar, arithmetic, ancient history, American history, English history, geography, literature, the sciences, more advanced math, Latin, a foreign language, music, and art. And this was what the schools provided.

No more, said Bobbitt and his fellow curriculum designers. Local school board members, teachers, and parents had not studied the new science of education. They knew little or nothing about IQ testing, about predicting future professions, or about tracking students correctly to make sure they would be prepared for their future careers. They were therefore as unqualified to design a school's curriculum as they were to criticize Einstein's theory of relativity. Both were jobs for trained experts.

Diane Ravitch is, today, a leading expert on the history of American education. In her book, *Left Back*, she says about this trend: "The invention of the scientific curriculum expert represented an extraordinary shift in power away from teachers, parents, and local communities to professional experts.... In modern school districts, control over curriculum was transferred from educators who had majored in English, history, or mathematics to trained curriculum experts."

What was the goal of these so-called scientists? Bobbitt and his colleagues thought of themselves as educational engineers who could figure out the best future profession for each child—they could find that "sweet spot" in which each child could most benefit society in the future.

The aim was not to educate children. It was to train them to serve society.

So, for example, if agricultural production fell off, the schools should provide better training in agriculture. If production lagged in American factories, then the schools must focus on industrial education. If studies showed a decline in American health, or many work days lost to illness, then the schools must teach health education. If the US military needed soldiers, then the schools must provide military training. If Americans were poor drivers, then the schools must teach driver's education…and so on. The focus should always be on practical benefits to society, not on teaching children to think.

How is it useful, Bobbitt asked, for students to read plays and poetry from hundreds of years earlier? How, for example, would it benefit a twentieth-century plumber to read *Macbeth* or *Hamlet* or Shakespeare's love poems? If the schools teach farmers the basic science necessary for them to grow crops, how would it help to also teach them physics or trigonometry or calculus? And why should they spend time learning Greek or Roman history? Or even the history of the American Revolution that occurred 125 to 150 years earlier? Why should future factory workers waste time studying grammar, learning sentence structure, and writing essays on a novel by Nathaniel Hawthorne? History, to the new curriculum designers, was largely a useless field (and soon to be replaced by "social studies").

Bobbitt's 1918 book, *Curriculum*, became for years the standard textbook on the subject in America's teachers' colleges.

Another influential curriculum designer, W.W. Charters at the Carnegie Institute of Technology, shared this view. He rejected the notion that children should study the works of "the masters." Such brilliant works of genius held little or no value for most Americans, he held. Ravitch quotes him: Curriculum designers should discover what "was most useful to the young in coping with the humble problems of their lives." The schools should figure out children's likely future professions and train them for it. For example, if a student most likely would become a department store clerk who specialized in credit applications, the schools should train him or her in practical skills such as friendliness, the ability to answer questions tactfully, a spirit of follow-up, keen judgment in answering credit questions, and so forth.

Momentum against intellectual training was building among American educators. It was about to become even stronger.

CHAPTER FOUR

The Curse of the CRSE

The year was 1912. The Bureau of Education was the forerunner of today's Department of Education. The US secretary of the interior demanded that the bureau thoroughly revise American schooling. Revise it from what? What was American schooling like at the turn of the twentieth century?

Charles Eliot of Harvard University provided a clue. In 1893, he headed the Commission of Ten, which reported on secondary education in the US. The commission was clear in its recommendations. Charles Sykes, in his book, *Dumbing Down Our Kids*, quotes Eliot: "As studies in language and in the natural sciences are best adapted to cultivate the habits of observation; as mathematics are the traditional training of the reasoning faculties…so history and its allied branches are better adapted than any other studies to promote the invaluable mental power which we call judgment." *The Commission of Ten recognized that training a student's mind to think effectively is the fundamental purpose of a proper education.*

This was the form of schooling that the Bureau of Education was ordered to thoroughly revise. The government agency partnered with the National Education Association (NEA). Jointly, they appointed the Commission on the Reorganization of Secondary Education (CRSE). The CRSE issued the new Cardinal Principles of Secondary Education in 1918. To this day, a full century later, it remains the most important document in modern American schooling.

The report stated that moving forward, the schools would "concern themselves less with academic matters than with the preparation for effective living"—that is, for playing one's part in a scientifically engineered society. This meant cutting down on courses that would enable students to think for themselves and expanding on courses that would teach them to pursue the common good.

The Seven Cardinal Principles

There were seven cardinal principles (main objectives) that the schools would then focus on. One was Health—the teaching of personal hygiene and emphasizing a "love for clean sport."

A second was Command of Fundamental Processes, which involved teaching basic thinking and learning skills. Professor Richard Mitchell, who became well-known as a writing and grammar expert, calling himself "the Underground Grammarian," commented in his book, *The Graves of Academe*: "About the other 'main objectives,' they have a lot to say.... When they have called for Command of Fundamental Processes, that's it. They proceed at once to *Worthy Home-membership*, a main objective much more to their liking." Because Command of Fundamental Processes was the only objective concerned with academic training, the progressive educators did not think it deserved any further explanation.

The third objective, as Mitchell noted, was Worthy Home-membership, which meant that every high school girl would be taught how to effectively run a household (regardless of whether she knew anything about math, history, literature, or science).

The fourth was Vocation, later known as industrial arts or shop class, which would teach blue-collar employment skills.

Fifth was Civics, which would largely replace history. It was here where the CRSE showed who it really was and what it really cared about. Charles Sykes writes about American education. His book *Dumbing Down Our Kids* is very good for anyone interested in understanding what has been done to American schooling. In it he states that the commissioners "who wrote the Cardinal Principles were especially uninterested in the US Constitution and the ideas of the Founding Fathers. Civics should concern itself less with Constitutional questions and [more] with... the informal activities of daily life that...seek the common good. Such agencies as child welfare organizations...afford specific opportunities for the expression of civic qualities."

Perhaps the most important thing about the Civics objective was that it continuously urged the students to perform group projects, emphasized that solutions were found by cooperation, encouraged group recitations, and so forth. Charles Sykes quoted the *Cardinal Principles*: All of these activities were intended to develop "a sense of collective responsibility....[and] training in collective thinking."

What does "training in collective thinking" mean? Strip away the fancy word "collective," which in simpler language means "to act as a group," and what do we have? We have the idea that individuals should not be encouraged to think for themselves, but rather that they should work within a group; they should discuss, argue, haggle, and, if necessary, compromise. They should go along with the consensus. And if one kid's own mind tells him or her that the group is wrong? Then that child should surrender his or her own judgment and conform to the group.

The sixth objective was Worthy Use of Leisure, which is based on two beliefs: 1. that most of us, without help from the schools, do not know how to relax and enjoy ourselves, and 2. that teaching kids how to have fun is a good use of school time.

The seventh and final objective was Ethical Character. This means that the schools—government-run agencies— were to teach morals to children. Even leaving aside the point that parents, not schools, should teach morals to their children, we are still left with the scary question: What moral code would government-run schools teach children? Given the CRSE's emphasis on collective thinking and collective responsibility, I think we have a good idea. They would teach conformity to the group and obedience to the state. They would not teach that it is good is to use one's own mind, to stand up for what one knows is right, or, if necessary, to question the authority of the government or of religious leaders.

In her book, *Left Back*, Diane Ravitch writes, "The driving purpose behind the seven objectives was socialization, teaching students to fit into society.... The overriding goal was social efficiency, not the realization of individual desire for self-improvement." When we talk about education, an individual's desire for self-improvement means to gain knowledge and to improve thinking skills. But the CRSE cared very little for this.

It should make our jaws drop that in 1918 the leading organization of American educators, to a large degree, stripped academic subjects out of the nation's schools. It saw very little need to train the mind. By contrast, let's remember some of the great accomplishments of many Americans before that year. Remember the great writings of Nathaniel Hawthorne, Edgar Allan Poe, Henry David Thoreau, Herman Melville, Mark Twain, and many others. Remember, too, the advances in technology made by Thomas Edison, Alexander Graham Bell, the Wright brothers, and other American geniuses, while at the same time at Harvard, William James pioneered the field of cognitive psychology. Let us not forget that at the turn of the twentieth century, innovative Americans created a film industry; commercialized radio; created jazz, blues, and Broadway musicals; developed a mass publishing industry, and would soon create television. I could go on with the inventions and new creations made by American thinkers during the nineteenth century and at the turn of the twentieth. But this is enough to make the point.

While brilliant American minds revolutionized one field after another, the country's leading educators were busy stripping most academic subjects from the core of the country's schooling. Charles Sykes writes in his book,

Dumbing Down Our Kids, "The Cardinal Principles, which are [talkative] to the point of [boredom] on every aspect of schooling, dismissed scholarship with a single sentence: 'Provisions should be made also for those having distinctly academic interests.' And that's it; the commission offered no further comment, suggestions, or guidelines." The academic parts of education were treated as unimportant, as an afterthought to the practical training the commissioners thought was really valuable. This philosophy soon started to dominate the schools of education…and it still does.

What a contrast with Charles Eliot and the Committee of Ten! They strongly advocated the study of history, science, math, literature, and other academic subjects. Recall the point from the last chapter: American parents overwhelmingly desired their children to master academic subjects (and they generally still do). Prior to the rise of the curriculum experts around the time of World War I, the US schools delivered the academic program desired by parents.

The End of History as a Subject

History was one academic field about to be severely dumbed down or even in many cases eliminated by the curriculum experts. Before the CRSE, most high schools offered (even required) a four-year program in history that covered ancient, European, English, and American history. But now, the CRSE invented a new field, called "social studies." History, according to the new curriculum designers, had little practical social value. But social studies would.

The CRSE was made up of sixteen (later seventeen) committees. The Committee on Social Studies was led by

Thomas Jesse Jones. Jones was a famous supporter of vocational training and one of the first to use the term "social studies." This new field was a hodgepodge of subjects that included some history. But mostly, in Diane Ravitch's words in *Left Back*, it would focus on "social efficiency, or teaching students the skills or attitudes necessary to fit into the social order." In other words, learning to conform to the majority was important. Learning history was not.

Civics, which is a field that studies government, was a part of the social studies curriculum…but was now changed to fit the new social activism. It was now not as important for children to learn how the president was elected as it was to understand the activities of the town dogcatcher. For example, in *Left Back*, Diane Ravitch quoted the Committee on Social Studies:

> *"The old chronicler who recorded the deeds of kings and warriors and neglected the labors of the common man is dead. The great palaces and cathedrals and pyramids are often but the empty shells of a parasitic growth on the working group. The elaborate descriptions of these old tombs are but sounding brass and tinkling cymbals compared to the record of joys and sorrows, the hopes and disappointments of the masses, who are infinitely more important than any arrangement of wood and stone and iron."*

Notice that the philosophy here is warmed-over Marxism. We see the emphasis on the masses or the group or the collective; we see the scorn for the activities of kings and rulers—which, for better or worse, often had a major impact on the lives of many human beings. Those activities included the positive things accomplished by leaders such as Julius Caesar, Augustus, Marcus Aurelius, and Napoleon. The emphasis on workers such as stonemasons, woodworkers, and ditch diggers would even exclude studying the deeds of men such as George Washington, Thomas Jefferson, Abraham Lincoln, and other American political leaders—an abysmal approach later resulting in the fact that zero of twenty college students in my class knew James Madison's role in authoring the United States Constitution and the Bill of Rights.

We also notice that the Committee on Social Studies scorned arrangements of wood and stone and iron—and yet such arrangements, and the people who created them, lifted human beings from caves to huts, to comfortable houses, to skyscrapers.

After this, history, to the degree it was taught at all, would focus on little guys, not great achievers, and would promote a single goal: fit into the social order—adjust, accept, conform. Teachers were to socialize the children, not to nurture a love of learning and thinking, or a curiosity about science, literature, math, or history. Along these lines, let us recall that during this same period, Harvard philosophy professor George Santayana famously remarked: "Those who cannot remember the past are condemned to repeat it." Perhaps Eliot and the Commission of Ten had a similar insight driving their support of teaching history. But the CRSE thoroughly rejected it.

Above all, teachers were not to develop in students an ability to think, learn, or function on their own. Whatever else progressive educators disagreed about, they agreed that independent thinking was wrong. The CRSE drove this anti-intellectual policy deep into the mainstream of US schooling.

The man who took the lead in spearheading the assault on academic education was John Dewey (1859–1952), a professor of philosophy at Columbia University. He exerted a powerful and terrible influence on American schooling.

CHAPTER FIVE

John Dewey - the Archvillain of American
Schooling

John Dewey was an unlikely figure to oversee the destruction of intellectual training in American schools. After all, he held a PhD in philosophy from Johns Hopkins University, taught philosophy for many years at the University of Chicago and Columbia University, wrote numerous books and essays, founded the legendary University of Chicago Laboratory School, where he and his wife taught academic subjects to children, and so on. He was not a curriculum designer trained in IQ tests and predicting students' future careers. Rather, he had a brilliant mind, was trained in a demanding academic discipline, and had a worldwide reputation as a lofty intellectual.

Yet Dewey was the main culprit responsible for destroying American education. If we wrote a historical novel dramatizing the fight to save US schooling, Dewey would be the story's villain.

From 1905 until 1930, Dewey was a star in Columbia University's philosophy department. From that perch he was a guide to leading progressive educators at Columbia's Teachers College, the major teacher training program in the US. He clearly made his point about academic training and independent thinking, writing in his book, *The School and Society*: "The mere absorbing of facts and truths is so exclusively individual an affair that it tends very naturally to pass into selfishness. There is no obvious social motive for the acquirement of mere learning, there is no clear social gain in success thereat."

Dewey was especially effective in promoting progressive education because he, in effect, mixed the poison with legitimate techniques of education. For example, he held that children learn best by experience, by choosing and engaging in hands-on projects. He helped popularize the idea that young students should engage in real-life activities that help them to gain practical skills. He believed, for instance, that children could learn reading while going through cookbooks, writing by jotting down a favorite recipe, and arithmetic by counting eggs and weighing flour. There is some truth in all of this.

Dewey, unlike many other progressives, did not entirely reject academic training. At the Laboratory School that he and his wife, Alice, founded and ran at the University of Chicago from 1896 to 1904, they taught a great deal of intellectual subject matter. Katherine Camp Mayhew and Anna Camp Edwards were experts on this part of Dewey's career. They wrote in their book, *The Laboratory School of the University of Chicago, 1896–1903*, "They [Dewey and his wife] continually experimented with different ways of [teaching] young students about primitive life in the

Bronze Age...early Greek civilization...Prince Henry of Portugal, Columbus, and other explorers...Shakespeare's plays; science; mathematics; algebra and geometry; English, French, and even Latin." Also, Diane Ravitch writes in *Left Back* that, in spite of his belief in learning by doing, Dewey "taught by standing in front of his class and lecturing."

But Dewey's primary aims were extremely harmful to American schooling. He wrote in *The School and Society* that all learning is ultimately for the purpose of "saturating [students] with the spirit of service." Dewey wrote a number of works on education. These include his book, *Experience and Education*, and his essay, "My Pedagogic Creed," as well as *The School and Society*. In them, he made clear that the purpose of education is not to transmit "bodies of information and skills that have been worked out in the past"—not to teach children "science, nor literature, nor history, nor geography"—but rather to prime them for "social cooperation and community life."

Dewey put his fame and influence behind the idea that schools should train children to fit into the social system rather than to learn intellectual content and think independently. His support also provided credibility to a small army of progressive educators who were vastly more opposed to academic training than even he was. The irony is thick: Dewey, the internationally famous philosopher, gave to the progressive movement's goal of eliminating intellectual training the sanction of "high-minded philosophy."

Dewey's Leading Disciple: William Heard Kilpatrick

The leading progressive educator influenced by Dewey was William Heard Kilpatrick (1871–1965).

Kilpatrick regarded himself as Dewey's leading disciple. For many years (1918 to 1940) he headed the philosophy of education department at Columbia University's Teachers College. From this influential position, he trained an estimated thirty-five thousand students, coming from every state in the country, at a time when Teachers College was training a large number of persons who went on to become America's leading educators. E.D. Hirsch Jr., author of *The Schools We Need and Why We Don't Have Them*, says: "Although the progressive movement in American education is often associated with John Dewey…the most influential introducer of progressive ideas into American schools of education was William Heard Kilpatrick."

Kilpatrick was the main force behind the "project method" of learning. He was a strong opponent of academic education, and he headed the Committee on the Problem of Mathematics for the CRSE. There, he argued that the teaching of math should, in general, be greatly cut down, and that students should be divided into groups. He believed that the only students who should study a great deal of math were the ones projected to be future scientists, engineers, and the like. He held that the rest, a huge majority of American students, should be taught little more than basic arithmetic even in high school.

Just as with Dewey, some of Kilpatrick's methods were actually effective in teaching. For example, he believed that very young children can advance quickly when allowed to choose and pursue their own hands-on projects. Diane Ravitch wrote in *Left Back* that the kinds of projects he supported were "a girl making a dress; a boy producing a school newspaper; a class presenting a play; a group of boys organizing a baseball team." Kilpatrick believed that this made education "like life itself," and not merely training for adult life. And this part of his methods makes sense.

But his overall goal, like Dewey's, was another matter. His project method was not designed to train students' minds, provide a great deal of knowledge, or encourage independent thinking. Rather, its purpose was to engineer social conformity.

Diane Ravitch in *Left Back* quotes Kilpatrick's essay, "The Project Method," and shows us his prime goal: "In contrast to the 'customary set-task sit-alone-at-your-own-desk procedure' which promotes 'selfish individualism,' the project method [involves] the pressure of social approval [which] would encourage conformity to 'the ideals necessary for approved social life.'"

Pilgrimages to the Soviet Union

It is not surprising that Kilpatrick admired Communism and visited the Soviet Union in 1929. He was very happy to see that the Communists put into practice his project method. In *Left Back*, Ravitch quotes a biography by Samuel Tenenbaum titled *William Heard Kilpatrick: Trailblazer in Education*. Tenenbaum wrote that Kilpatrick observed groups of students "disposing of disintegrating carcasses of animals left frozen by the roadside." The Columbia education professor said enthusiastically that "no school system in history has been more thoroughly and consistently made to work into the social and political program of the state."

Dewey also pilgrimaged to the Soviet Union and admired what he saw there. Ravitch writes about Dewey's response: He reported that the Soviet educators "realized that the goals of the progressive school were undermined by 'the egoistic and private ideals and methods inculcated by the institution of private property, profit, and acquisitive possession.'" He recognized that Communist propaganda was everywhere in the country, but he excused it because it served "the good of humanity" rather than selfish private gain. He even expressed some praise for the Communist attempt to do away with the family unit, which was in keeping with the Marxist theory that a family unit is individualistic, selfish, and hostile to communal living.

George Counts, an early disciple of Dewey's and another educator at Columbia University's Teachers College, was even more generous with his praise of Communism. Twice he visited the Soviet Union, and he became convinced that American schools must take the lead in changing the United States from a capitalist to a socialist state. Counts intended to turn progressive education into political activism in support of socialism.

Progressive educators had long held a hodgepodge of theories. On the one hand, they believed that children's impulses should guide their schooling, that they should do what they felt like, that every child should, in effect, do his own thing. On the other, they believed that the purpose of education was to socialize children—to teach them to conform and fit into the social order. These two approaches did not clash as much as they seemed to. For whether children were encouraged to act on their desires or taught to conform to the group, or, under different circumstances, to do both, they were never taught to *think independently*. Under the Communism admired by progressives, what is the political fate of those who know next to nothing and who cannot think? The conformists will obey the all-powerful state. The persons who have regard only for their desires, who have been taught to follow their own urges, will be crushed by the totalitarian state. Or they will learn to obey, now following the desires of the dictator rather than their own.

Counts was very clear about what the political goals of the progressive movement in education should be. He wrote a book titled *Dare the Schools Build a New Social Order?* Diane Ravitch says in *Left Back* that Counts "forthrightly called for elimination of capitalism, property rights, private profit, and competition, and establishment of collective ownership of natural resources, capital, and the means of production and distribution." In order to indoctrinate children with the ideals of Communism, he called for the classroom to be completely socialized. He accused the so-called *child-centered* progressives of having no social theory "unless it be that of anarchy and extreme individualism." He rejected the notion that education can "build its program out of the interests of the children," and claimed that America must become "less frightened than it is today at the bogeys of imposition and indoctrination."

This was the Depression era, and Counts' message was well received. Ravitch points out that almost all of the major progressives of the 1930s believed that the traditional academic curriculum reflected what they considered to be a failed capitalist political-economic system.

They were wrong that capitalism was (or is) a failed system. In truth, it provides far more freedom and prosperity than the full socialism they supported. Any study of Cold War history and/or current events shows us this. Take Venezuela's semi-capitalist past versus its Communist present, for example. Or Cuba versus the Cuban-American community in Miami. Or China's attempt to impose Communist dictatorship on Hong Kong. Or North Korea versus South Korea. Or the Cold War struggle of the USSR versus the USA. By the measures of freedom and prosperity, capitalism always wins.

But in a twisted way, the progressives were right that academic subjects in education and capitalism in politics and economics go together. Capitalism, rightly understood, is a system that protects individual rights. It is a system that protects an individual's "inalienable right to life, liberty, and the pursuit of happiness." In the capitalist system, an individual's life belongs to the individual, not to the state. And when the principle of individual rights is universally applied, as it should be, it protects the rights of women and minorities, not just those of white males.

Here is the connection to academic subjects in education: Effective training in them provides students with both knowledge and thinking skills. Reading, writing, and the ability to calculate in arithmetic and higher forms of math are thinking skills. This type of education enables individuals to think for themselves; it makes them more independent. They can understand for themselves what is true and what is false, what is right and what is wrong. They are less likely to go along with what the group believes, less likely to accept some false or horribly wrong claim just to win acceptance from their peers. They are much less likely to obey a Communist (or a Fascist) totalitarian state.

Similarly, the capitalist system protects political independence—the legal right to think for oneself, to express oneself, and to live for one's own happiness. It follows that if people want to destroy political independence in favor of Communism, as the progressives did, one way to do so is to destroy intellectual independence. Independent thinkers will direct their own lives, as adults properly do, rather than being taken care of by the state, as are children by their parents. They will think independently and often question authority; they will not blindly obey. The progressives recognized that to build a society of nonthinkers who would be obedient to the state, they must begin by building a classroom that requires conformity to the group.

The progressives and their modern heirs severely dumbed down American schools as a necessary means to impose conformity, dependency, and obedience. Their vision is clear: They, the educated, intellectual elite—the educational and social engineers—will govern in the classroom and in the legislature. The rest of us will conform and obey.

Fortunately, this vision was not shared by all educators.

CHAPTER SIX

Educational Supporters of Literacy and Learning

The time was 1884; the place was Rome. A fourteen-year-old Italian girl adamantly refused her parents' suggestion that she become a teacher. She was fascinated by mathematics, and she wanted to become an engineer. She was undaunted by people continually informing her that young ladies did not go into the field of engineering and felt similarly several years later when she changed her allegiance to medicine. The director of the Board of Education in Rome told her it would be impossible for her to become a medical doctor. The male students harassed her. Her own father disapproved. But she thanked the director respectfully and quietly told him that she was certain she would become a Doctor of Medicine. She became the first female medical student in Italian history. Many years later, a medical professor at the university, now very old, told this story: One winter day, there was a terrible blizzard in Rome. None of the other students made it to his lecture. There was only one person in the auditorium, his female student. She politely suggested that he postpone his lecture. No, he said. Such dedication must be rewarded. He gave the lecture to her alone. Such dedication to her goals enabled the student, Maria Montessori, to eventually revolutionize childhood education. E. M. Standing, in his biography, *Maria Montessori: Her Life and Work*, tells this story vividly.

Montessori's Method

Maria Montessori (1872–1950) developed revolutionary methods of training a child's mind. Her ideas entered US education during the early twentieth century, at around the same time as the progressives were taking over the American schools.

Maria Montessori understood that the proper task of education is to develop a child's mind.

She understood that our thinking begins in sensory experience, with our powers of observation, with our eyes, ears, nose, and sense of touch. She created exercises to train young students to engage and cultivate their senses, to develop their motor skills—that is, their movements, bodily coordination, and hand-eye coordination, and to be able to concentrate for long periods of time. She scaled down classroom furniture and materials to child size, making it easier for children to use them.

She taught young children to read using the method of phonics—teaching them the letters of the alphabet, the sounds of all the letters and the combinations of letters, and how to sound out the letters of the words on the printed page. And in this way, she unlocked for them the worlds of literature, history, and science. She also taught them to write and to do basic arithmetic as well as fractions, decimals, and geometry.

In contrast to the progressives, Montessori encouraged the students in her classroom to work on their own, using her materials. Often, the students worked by themselves on the subjects they chose and with materials they chose. The children could team up and work together if they chose to, but the main rule in Montessori's classroom was, in effect: Thou shalt not disturb a child doing his or her own work.

So, for example, if a young girl was deeply involved in reading a history book and one of the boys who had read the book approached her and offered to discuss it with her, it was up to the girl to choose if she wanted to keep reading by herself or discuss it with her fellow student. Montessori taught her students to always respect the choices of their peers, to respect each other's privacy and work time, and to never disrupt a student at work. In this way, she taught the children that they were individuals, each one valuable, and that they could join together in cooperation if they chose to but did not have to submit to the will of the group. They did not have to conform.

As part of growing into responsible adults, the children were responsible for cleaning up after themselves, for tidying the classroom at the end of the day, often for taking care of animals and/or plants, for baking and/or cooking meals, and for mastering other practical life skills.

In the years prior to World War I, Montessori's methods started to catch on in the United States. The first American Montessori school was founded in 1911 in Tarrytown, New York, and was soon followed by others. Her book on education, *The Montessori Method*, was translated from her native Italian into English and quickly sold through a number of editions. Alexander Graham Bell (inventor of the telephone) and his wife publicly supported her methods. In 1913, she visited the United States and spoke around the country, generally to large and enthusiastic crowds. *McClure's Magazine*, a widely read publication of the day, featured a series of articles on her methods. During this period, just over one hundred years ago, Montessori's methods held out a great deal of promise for the future of American schooling.

The Great Books Program

Shortly after that, in the 1920s, a pair of American educators rejected the antiacademic bias that was starting to dominate the educational establishment. Similar to Montessori, but from a different angle, these men proposed a new, highly academic program for training the minds of students. Robert Maynard Hutchins and Mortimer J. Adler were the two rebel leaders of this new movement. Hutchins was the young president of the University of Chicago. Adler was a determined autodidact (a self-taught person). He was possibly the only person in history who gained a PhD (in psychology from Columbia University) without holding either a high school diploma or an undergraduate degree.

Together, these two led a vigorous campaign on behalf of what they called the Great Books program. Hutchins and Adler believed that an outstanding education required mastering the great books, the classic works of Western civilization, and that such academic training was the proper purpose of education.

For students to take on such difficult works—to read Aristotle, Galileo, and Shakespeare, for instance—in high school and college, they needed a solid grounding in academic subjects. Years later, in the 1980s, Adler published a series of guidelines designed to improve American schooling. He strongly suggested an end to the progressives' tracking and dividing of children, and to a mere handful receiving full academic education while the rest were assigned to vocational training.

Adler developed what he called a "Paideia" Program in education, taking the name from the ancient Greek ideal of educating a student's mind, body, and character. The editors of the *Encyclopedia Britannica* write this in their entry about Adler: He believed that "a single elementary and secondary school program for all students would ensure the upgrading of the curriculum and the quality of instruction to serve the needs of the brightest and to [educationally] lift the…least advantaged." He proposed that "vocational…training be given only after students had been given a full course of basic education in the humanities, arts, sciences, and language."

Starting in the late 1920s and continuing through the 1930s, Hutchins and Adler taught a class called Great Books of the Western World at the University of Chicago and other places. The reading list was made up of a Who's Who of Western history's greatest writers, philosophers, scientists, and mathematicians. Their students read, for example, Plato, Euclid, Galileo, Shakespeare, Johan Wolfgang von Goethe, Albert Einstein, and Sigmund Freud, and numerous other great minds.

Hutchins opposed vocational training in education. He claimed that an employer could train a thinking person in vocational skills in a matter of weeks on the job. In *Left Back*, Ravitch writes that for Hutchins "the object of general education should be 'the training of the mind'…. The kind of educational program that was needed…would teach students to appreciate the importance of ideas, to understand history, the fine arts and literature, and to grasp the principles of science."

This has always made sense to me. We're all human beings, after all; we have a human brain and a rational mind, and our mind must be trained in thinking and in the important themes of academic subjects. Adler and Hutchins are correct that those who desire careers needing vocational training can get it on the job. Or perhaps the last year in high school should be devoted to vocational training for those who want it. Or maybe it should be left to parents, extended family members, and/or vocational schools attended at night, on the weekends, or during the summer. Whichever one of these alternatives is accepted, thinking, knowledgeable, and motivated people can readily learn their chosen trade from someone experienced in the field. They will then be prepared to succeed and also will be proficient in academic subjects.

This reminds me that as a kid in Brooklyn, I had a friend (call him Chris) with whom I played a lot of basketball in the local park. He was a bus mechanic. He was a damn good mechanic. He loved his work, which I can understand, because there is a lot of satisfaction in making broken stuff work again. As a highly skilled worker, he also made a good deal of money. Nevertheless, Chris attended Kingsborough Community College, taking one or two classes at night per semester. It took him several years to get his two-year degree. Then he went on to Brooklyn College. All in all, it took him eight or ten years to get his four-year liberal arts degree.

His fellow bus mechanics at work noticed him carrying copies of Shakespeare's plays, or Dostoyevsky's novels, or an album (or CD) of Beethoven's piano sonatas, and were surprised. Such highbrow stuff was generally not their cup of tea. "You're a bus mechanic," they said. "Why are you reading (or listening to) this stuff?" Chris' response was simple: "I'm a bus mechanic. That doesn't mean I have to be an uneducated bus mechanic." Indeed, it doesn't.

Hutchins was a young, brilliant, well-spoken supporter of intellectual training, and his message was enthusiastically received by newspapers, magazines, parents, and the general public.

But not by the schools of education.

CHAPTER SEVEN

The Enemies of Intellectual Training Attack

William Heard Kilpatrick leaped immediately to battle stations. He was not a man to waste time—he was a man on a mission—and he led the assault on the pro-academic educators.

Kilpatrick recognized the dangers to progressive education posed by Montessori's methods, and immediately responded to her challenge. In 1914, he published a critical booklet, "The Montessori System Examined." In it, he rejected Montessori's methods, claiming that they offered nothing in education that was both new and correct. Among his many criticisms, the most important was his objection to academic training introduced at such at an early age. He made the narrow criticism that phonics was an effective method to teach reading in the Italian language but was not right for English, in which a number of words are not phonetic. To illustrate Kilpatrick's point, even a simple word like "rough" is not pronounced the way it is spelled. To have the spelling match the pronunciation, the word should be spelled "ruff." But it isn't. Kilpatrick emphasized that there are many such words in the English language. Therefore, he concluded, phonics is not a good method to teach reading in this language.

More broadly, Kilpatrick rejected academic subjects as not right for children who are three to five years old. He wrote that education is much more than the gaining of knowledge from books. He was so opposed to book learning at an early age that he claimed even the mere presence of books in a child's early schooling makes other, more important parts of education more difficult. He claimed that reading and writing should be postponed to a later period in a child's life. He believed that intellectual training at an early age distracted a child from more important parts of life—and he held that academics should not be included during the kindergarten period.

Attacks on the Great Books Approach

In the same way, Kilpatrick was brutal in his criticism of Hutchins, Adler, and the Great Books program. He contrasted Hutchins with William Bagley, a fellow progressive who was less opposed to academic training than Kilpatrick and most progressives. Diane Ravitch says in *Left Back*: "Bagley annoyed Progressive educators but Robert Maynard Hutchins drove them into a rage…. Unthinkable, his claim that the purpose of education was intellectual training." Ravitch minces no words when she describes Kilpatrick's rage toward the Great Books supporters:

> *William Heard Kilpatrick was…horrified by*
> *Hutchins' views. He fulminated [exploded—*

> *in this sense, verbally] that Hutchins was an authoritarian whose ideas were out of step with "every intellectual advance of the last 300 years." Worse, "Dr. Hutchins stands near to Hitler. When you have a professed absolute, then you have to have some authority to give it content, and there the dictator comes in."*

Dewey also ripped the Great Books supporters. Dewey, let us remember, was a leading philosopher of the pragmatist school, a school of thought developed in the United States around the turn of the twentieth century. He and other pragmatists believed that change was constant, and that things that were true during ancient or medieval times were not necessarily true in the modern world. Events move us forward, circumstances change, and we must be prepared to challenge and perhaps change every belief we hold, including sacred ones. To put it in more philosophic terms, there are no absolutes. So every belief is therefore subject to testing, scientific experimentation, endless revision, and being proved false. Dewey, like Kilpatrick, also compared Hutchins to the 1930s dictators who were terrorizing Europe at the time.

Ravitch writes:

> *Dewey went so far as to imply that Hutchins was ideologically linked with the jackbooted thugs who were then brutalizing Europe. "I would not intimate that*

the author [Hutchins] has any sympathy
with Fascism. But basically, his idea as
to the proper course to be taken is akin to
the distrust of freedom and the consequent
appeal to some fixed authority that is now
over-running the world."

To many honest persons, Kilpatrick's and Dewey's criticisms of the Great Books approach is puzzling. After all, Hutchins and Adler wanted students to read books of not just one philosophic or scientific tradition. Rather, they wanted students to read countless great books, from a wide variety of thinkers, from many different countries, from every era and time period. Some of the books were religious and some were not; some were even antireligious. The various philosophers whose works were to be read were of many different, even opposing schools of thought. It was the same for the works of the various scientists to be studied.

Kilpatrick's charge that the Great Books approach was out of step with "every intellectual advance of the last 300 years" is especially puzzling, because Hutchins and Adler wanted students to read the books of John Locke, Isaac Newton, Goethe, Voltaire, Immanuel Kant, Charles Darwin, Einstein, Freud, and numerous other geniuses of the previous 300 years—that is, the great minds largely responsible for the advances made in the past three centuries.

Even more disturbing is the twisted logic and brutal irony of *Soviet admirers* claiming support for totalitarianism on the part of those seeking to nurture *independent thinking*. The intellectual training and independent thinking urged by the Great Books supporters are directly opposite the obedience and conformity demanded under a dictatorship. The truth is that Dewey, Kilpatrick, Counts, and other progressives supported Communism, a form of brutal dictatorship; Adler and Hutchins did not.

How did John Dewey, a world-famous philosopher, come to despise an educational approach based on the study of many of history's greatest philosophers? Among the many reasons is that Dewey and the progressives confused intellectual certainty with political authority and a push toward dictatorship. Is it accurate to say that if we are certain of truths, we will then push toward dictatorship to make people accept them? If we have no doubts, for example, that 3 x 3 = 9, or that George Washington was the first president of the United States, or that on Earth, the law of gravity holds true, or that many other such claims are likewise true, does this mean that we will inevitably sic the Gestapo on people who reject them? Such a belief is clearly false, for why don't we clamor for the arrest of the Flat Earthers who deny the well-proven claim that the Earth is round?

To hold the above truths (and many others) as absolutes is a basis for understanding nature and society. It is not a basis for political dictatorship.

Above all, Hutchins and Adler favored academic training for all students in order to develop their minds, to teach them to think for themselves, and, when necessary, to challenge authority. Kilpatrick and Dewey, on the other hand, admirers of Soviet Communism *during Stalin's reign*, were supporters of the very type of dictatorship they claimed to reject.

Perhaps it is the case that the progressives recognized this and rejected the Great Books approach because of it. Maybe they realized that independent thinkers would not conform to the group, would not blindly obey the group's leaders, and would not accept the Communist dictatorship that the progressives admired.

The battle lines between these two groups of educators were clearly drawn. One group wanted to teach elementary school children practical life skills and conformity, with a small amount of academic education mixed in. The other side also wanted to provide students with practical life skills, but with much academic teaching mixed in—and, above all, to teach the children how to think.

The differences continued into the high schools. One side wanted to socialize students, to teach vocational courses to the great majority and academic education only to an elite few. The other side wanted to continue teaching academic subjects to everyone, to teach students to think independently—and, in many cases, to prepare them to study the great works of Western Civilization, which shed light on history, literature, philosophy, and art, and provide valuable insights that thoughtful persons can use to guide their lives.

In short, the progressives wanted to fill the students with the spirit of service and prepare them for community life. Montessori, Hutchins, and Adler, on the other hand, wanted to teach students to think, learn, and understand the world.

In order to achieve their goals, progressives had to do more than attack the ideas of the educators who opposed them. Their campaign against academic education would lead them to attack the very root of intellectual development. What was the most effective way to prevent millions of students from receiving intellectual training? Cripple their ability to read.

CHAPTER EIGHT

The Great Reading Wars

Rudolf Flesch struck a mighty blow in support of effective reading in America.

Flesch (1911–1986) was an Austrian Jew who fled from the Nazis and immigrated to America. He held a doctorate in law from the University of Vienna and a PhD in library science from Columbia University. He knew there were few reading problems in Austria and in Western Europe generally. He was disturbed by the severe reading problems he encountered in the United States. In 1955, when the campaign in favor of academic education seemed lost, Flesch fired a shot heard round the nation when he published his brilliant book *Why Johnny Can't Read*.

Flesch wrote his book for American parents. He reached out to them about, among other things, remedial instruction for struggling readers. He writes: "[T]here are no remedial reading cases in Austrian schools…. There are no remedial reading cases in Germany, in France, in Italy, in Norway, in Spain…practically anywhere in the world except in the United States… Did you know that there was no such thing as remedial reading in this country either until about thirty years ago?"

Flesch discovered that beginning in the early twentieth century, American educators generally rejected the tried-and-true phonics method of teaching reading. Phonics makes good use of one of the great advances of human civilization: the development of the Roman alphabet. This alphabet is the basis of most European languages. It is made up of twenty-six letters that give rise to forty-four sounds in English. By the time most children reach five years of age, they can generally speak thousands of words in their mother tongue. At this point (and probably earlier) it is possible to teach them the alphabet. These are the literary shapes (or symbols) that visually stand for the verbal sounds. What is known as systematic phonics, let us recall, involves teaching beginning readers the letters of the alphabet and all of the sounds they make in combination. In a matter of months, children between the ages of five and six (and probably younger) can learn the letters and all of the sounds, and begin to sound out words. For centuries, billions of children around the world have learned the all-important art of reading by this simple method.

This is true even in English, which is a so-called "irregular" language. "Irregular" means that some words are pronounced differently than they are spelled. A simple example is the word "tough." If it were phonetic, it would be spelled "tuff." But it isn't. Only about 13 percent of English words are pronounced differently than they are spelled. This means that roughly 87 percent of English words are phonetic. So children who are trained in phonics can sound out the great majority of words in the English language. Then, as effective readers, they can learn to match irregular spellings such as "one" or "enough" or "bought" with the spoken words they know well. They do this by determining what makes sense in the context of the sentence or by asking their teacher or a parent.

The Whole Word Method

But for most of the twentieth century and into the twenty-first, most US educators rejected and are still rejecting phonics, preferring some version of the whole-word method, as mentioned earlier. This method does not teach children to look at the letters of a word and then to sound it out. Rather, it teaches them to look at the whole word, to try to recognize the shape of the word, to look at the context in which the word is used, and, if necessary, to guess.

The first version of this method was known as the look-say approach. Look-say supporters claimed that children learned to read by seeing a word over and over again. The theory was that children need master only a handful of commonly used words and then use context cues to figure out the rest. Using this method, it would be a disaster to overload the children with thousands of new word shapes at the beginning. Therefore, the look-say method introduces the students to only several hundred new words per year, beginning in first grade, and these are continuously repeated. Flesch quotes from a book commonly used to teach reading:

> *"We will look," said Susan. "Yes, yes," said all the children. "We will look and we will*

find it." So all the boys and girls looked.
They looked and looked for it. But they did
not find it.

There is one gigantic problem with this method. It is estimated that there are some 170,000 words currently in use in English, and that-native born adult English speakers have vocabularies somewhere in the range of twenty thousand to thirty-five thousand words. To put it simply: Nobody can memorize the shape of twenty thousand or more words. What will students who are not taught to sound out the letters do when they come upon words that have unfamiliar shapes? Suppose they come upon the sentence "The family toured the Gettysburg battlefield" and don't know the written words "battlefield" and "Gettysburg." Students trained in phonics could easily sound out these words and keep on reading. But students untrained in phonics would be stumped. They are taught to do the only thing they can do in this situation: guess.

And they are supposed to be praised for making a good guess, even if it is completely wrong. So, in the case of the above sentence, if children guess "The family toured the Galveston ballfield," they would be praised for making a good guess. After all, "Gettysburg battlefield" and "Galveston ballfield" are faintly similar in the shapes of the words.

Philosopher Leonard Peikoff, in his essay, "The American School: Why Johnny Can't Think," quotes an advocate of this method, Dixie Lee Spiegel. She writes of this method that children "should receive praise for a good guess even if it is not completely accurate. For example, if a child reads 'I like to eat carrots' as 'I like to eat cake,' praise should be given for supplying a word that makes sense and follows at least some of the phonic cues." Peikoff responded, "How would you like to see, at the head of our army, a general with this kind of schooling? He receives a telegram [today an instant message] from the president during a crisis ordering him to 'reject nuclear option,' proceeds to make a good guess, and reads it as 'release nuclear option.' Linguistically, the two are as close as 'carrots' and 'cake.'"

Supporters of the look-say method claim that phonics overloads a child's mind with too many letters and sounds that must be memorized. So instead, they uphold a system that requires students to *memorize the shape of every word in the language.* Memorize not just twenty-six letters and forty-four sounds that enable readers to sound out thousands of words in written English, but memorize the shape of every word in the entire language. Nobody, not the world's greatest genius, can do this, and this is why the look-say method is a terrible failure as a way to teach reading.

Phonics saves time and mental space. Once mastered, it's a simple method to decode the vast majority of words in the language. Look-say (or any version of the whole-word method), on the other hand, is like a huge warehouse containing thousands of items, all stored at random, with no lettered grouping, requiring searchers to memorize the shape of each box, later to recall that shape when searching for a particular item. It is no wonder that in practice, one method is much more successful than the other.

As mentioned, phonics was the dominant method in early US history. New Englanders used the *New England*

Primer (first published in 1690), and later, Americans employed Noah Webster's *Blue-Backed Speller* (first published in 1783). These textbooks used phonics to teach reading and were highly effective. Later, in the 19th century, *McGuffey's Readers* were suitable for both phonics and the whole-word method, but the large majority of Americans chose to employ phonics.

But by the 1920s, the professional curriculum designers had rejected phonics for look-say. For example, Arthur Gates of Teachers College at Columbia University, published a book in 1928 called *New Methods in Primary Reading*. It became an influential book rejecting phonics and supporting look-say. Flesch quotes an earlier essay in which Gates wrote: "That it will be the part of wisdom to curtail the phonetic instruction in the first grade very greatly, is strongly implied; indeed, it is not improbable that it should be eliminated entirely." His book argued along similar lines but watered down this advice slightly, leaving out the part about doing away with phonics altogether.

By the 1930s, look-say had become the major method in the teachers' colleges, in the textbooks, and in many schools. The infamous Dick and Jane readers had become the dominant textbooks for teaching reading to American children, and remained so for decades. For many years, children were bombarded with watered-down nonsense such as:

> *"See Spot run," said Jane. "See Spot run to the new house."*

> *"Come home, Spot," said Dick. "Come, Spot, come. Come home."*

When children are not taught to read by sounding out a word's letters, this kind of simple-minded hash, with a limited number of small words that are repeated endlessly, is all that they can be expected to read. Excellent children's books with good stories, such as *The Secret Garden*, will be beyond them.

By contrast, here is part of a story chosen at random from McGuffey's First Reader:

> *"Oh Hattie, I just saw a large rat in the shed; and old Nero tried to catch it."*

> *"Did he catch it, Frank?"*

> *"No, Nero did not; but the old cat did."*

> *"My cat?"*

> *"No, it was the other one."*

> *"Do tell me how she got it, Frank. Did she run after it?"*

> *"No, that was not the way. Puss was hid on a big box. The rat stole out, and she jumped at it and caught it."*

> *"Poor rat! It must have been very hungry; it came out to get something to eat."*

> *"Why, Hattie, you are not sorry puss got the rat, are you?"*

*"No, I cannot say I am sorry she got it; but I
do not like to see even a rat suffer pain."*

Notice what children get when they are taught to focus
on letters and sound out words: 1. a much more extensive
vocabulary employed in a first reader; 2. lessons in punc-
tuation—notice the correct use of semicolons to connect
independent clauses; 3. a more sophisticated story, and 4.
a moral theme: Although we do not like to inflict pain on
living beings, we still need to rid the house and the barnyard
of rodents.

By the 1950s, the whole-word method had been dominant in American schools for two decades...with disastrous
results. It was in this context that Flesch's book sounded
the alarm. It was made available in newspapers and magazines, and quickly became a bestseller in book form. It
just as quickly was rejected by the schools of education.
For millions of parents and thoughtful Americans, it was a
wake-up call and motivated them to campaign for phonics.
In that book and in later writings, Flesch devoted much
attention to showing and examining the results of tests that
pitted systematic phonics against the whole-word method.
In every test, students trained in phonics read better than
students trained in some version of the whole-word method.

One example of several that Flesch cited was a review of
numerous experiments conducted in the teaching of reading
by Robert Dykstra, professor of education at the University
of Minnesota. In 1973, Dykstra reviewed fifty-nine studies
on this issue. Flesch, in his later book, *Why Johnny Still Can't
Read*, summarized Dykstra's findings:

> [C]hildren get off to a faster start in reading if they are given early direct systematic instruction in the alphabetic code. The evidence clearly demonstrates that children who receive early intensive instruction in phonics develop superior word recognition skills in the early stages of reading and tend to maintain their superiority at least through the third grade.... We can summarize the results of 60 years of research dealing with beginning reading instruction by stating that early systematic instruction in phonics provides the child with the skills necessary to become an independent reader at an earlier age than is likely if phonics instruction is delayed and less systematic.

Also in 1961, the Carnegie Corporation of New York commissioned Jeanne Chall of the Harvard Graduate School of Education to research the issue and to finally resolve the dispute. In her 1967 book *Learning to Read*, she concluded: "For a beginning reader...knowledge of letters and sounds had more influence on reading achievement than the child's tested 'mental ability' or IQ."

In *Left Back*, Diane Ravitch writes, "Flesch's polemic set off a national debate about literacy.... Because of its popularity, Flesch's book had a swift and large effect on the teaching of reading." As a result, a number of publishers began to issue a new series of reading texts that used phonics as their main method.

The So-Called "Whole Language" Method is a Version of Whole Word

Nevertheless, the schools of education clung to the whole-word method—and by the 1980s, they launched a sweeping counterattack on phonics. They called the new version of the whole-word method the "whole-language" approach. Whole-language retained the whole-word approach. Phonics, once again, was out.

Some supporters of this approach, to their credit, understand that when children are introduced to great works of literature, they are motivated by their natural curiosity to want to read interesting stories. However, by rejecting phonics for this latest trendy version of the whole-word method, they end up crippling the students' ability to read great stories.

Martin Gross wrote an excellent book on American education titled *The Conspiracy of Ignorance*. One topic he addressed was the frustration of students during the 1980s and early 1990s when "taught" by this method. In his comments he quotes from an essay critical of the whole-language approach published in a journal of the American Federation of Teachers. Gross writes that "in whole language, millions of youngsters nationwide were surrounded by 'beautiful pieces of literature that they can't read.'"

Unfortunately for California children, the state became a testing ground for the whole-language method in the late 1980s and 1990s. By 1992, after this had been the dominant method in the California schools for several years, the NAEP held statewide reading tests. A shocking 52 percent of California's fourth graders were reading below the baseline set up for that grade. The whole-language approach was continued, however—and when the same test was given again two years later, 56 percent of California's fourth graders were reading below grade level. In *The Conspiracy of Ignorance* Gross quotes a teacher in the Los Angeles area who gave a heartbreaking report of first graders asked to read: "The children were in tears.... They look at you with three paragraphs on a page and they say, 'What do we do with this?'"

When some schools changed course and reintroduced phonics, the results were predictable: For example, after students taught via the whole-word method repeatedly tested poorly, their school in Texas switched to systematic phonics instruction. On a later statewide test, 98 percent of those students read at grade level or above.

The continued opposition to phonics on the part of many education professors would be beyond understanding if we assumed that their goal was to teach young children to read effectively. But when we understand their basic motives, the mystery disappears: Their goal is not to nurture independent thinkers but to create skilled workers obedient to the wise rulers of the state. If you want children to read well, you embrace phonics. If you do not want children to read well, or at all, you reject it. If you want students to master academic subjects, you embrace phonics. If you do not want students to master academic subjects, you reject it. If you want students to grow up as independent adults, guiding their own lives by use of their own minds, you use phonics to teach reading, and you emphasize reading, writing, math, and other academic subjects as the basics of education. But if you want students to grow up to be good at their vocation, to not think too much, to conform to society, and to serve the state, then you devalue both phonics and academic subjects in general.

It is no wonder that many American students cannot read effectively. The educational "experts" who train their teachers do not want them to.

CHAPTER NINE

Dumbing Down the Rest of the Curriculum

Here are a few more true horror stories from the front lines of education.

I was teaching Aristotle's ethics to my philosophy students. Aristotle was from Macedonia, whose location was unknown to all twenty-two students in the class. I mentioned that Alexander, a student of Aristotle's, had conquered the mighty Persian Empire. Only two knew that Persia is present-day Iran, and only four could find it on the map. So much for geography.

Regarding literature, everyone knew who Shakespeare was and that he'd written *Macbeth* and *Hamlet*; more than half the class even knew he'd written *Romeo and Juliet*. Six out of twenty-two knew that Nathaniel Hawthorne had written *The Scarlet Letter*, sixteen did not, two had read it, and nobody had heard of Charles Dickens. Regarding history, two had heard of Patrick Henry, but none knew what he was famous for—they were ignorant of his "Give me liberty or give me death!" speech—and none knew when he lived. My colleagues in the math department also tell me they often do a good deal of remedial work before the students are ready for college-level material. And the beat goes on.

The academic curriculum in American schools has been severely dumbed down. We know why. In keeping with the ideas of the curriculum designers and the progressive educators, less and less attention is given to academic subjects.

Math and Science

Regarding the teaching of math, for example, the writer Martin Gross reported in his book *The Conspiracy of Ignorance* that American middle schools are "heavily mired down in simple arithmetic" and rarely advance beyond it. By the late 1990s, only three states required more than two years of math to graduate from a public high school. Most of them required only two years—and a few others even less. By then, more than a third of public high school graduates had never taken a full course in basic algebra, 45 percent had never taken intermediate algebra, and trigonometry had all but vanished, with only one graduate in eight having taken an introductory course in the subject. The numbers have not changed much since then, and most high school graduates still do not know enough math to prepare them for college. Newspaper and magazine articles written by math professors testify to this sad truth; my colleagues in math and science departments bemoan it; and standardized test scores in math keep getting worse—or at best remain stagnant at a low level.

In the sciences, the story is much the same. While over 90 percent of high school kids study biology, only slightly more than half take a chemistry course, and less than a quarter study physics. Gross reports in *The Conspiracy of Ignorance*, "Only 20 percent of public high school graduates—one in five—take all three basic science courses."

Geography

I have only briefly mentioned the important field of geography. For many years, geography was taught in the US elementary and junior high schools. Gross reminds us that most schoolrooms used to have world maps, maps of every continent, and maps of the United States on the wall. Students learned the location of many countries. When called upon, they could go to the map and pick out Turkey or Australia or many other countries. They knew the locations of major rivers too, such as the Nile and the Amazon. They learned where the Himalayan Mountains, the Alps, and other mountain ranges are. They learned the names and locales of every state in our country, and in most cases, the names of the state capitals.

Sadly, that is no longer the case. As Gross writes in *The Conspiracy of Ignorance*, "[G]eography has long since been replaced by social studies, a grab-bag discipline that can cover *anything* the teacher and the school desire, including ecology, community relations, sex and race relations, history, geography, or whatever." Modern educators are often opposed to having students memorize facts. This kind of information bores students, they claim, and clutters their minds with too many details, so today, the schools often ignore the field of geography. But geography is knowledge of *our world*; it is knowing the globe and the various nations that make it up. For example, is it even possible to understand Chinese culture without knowing the country's location, the nature of its terrain, its rivers and mountains, its climate, its major crops, and so forth? Obviously not. And today, American kids stare blankly when asked the location of Iran or North Korea or even Russia, nations that aren't merely important but that may pose a danger to American lives.

In *The Conspiracy of Ignorance*, Gross quotes Osa Brand, who was president of the Association of American Geographers. She says: "When social studies came about in the public schools, geography fell by the wayside." She notes the poor performance by American kids in geography on the NAEP tests, especially when contrasted with how well European kids generally do. The reason for this, she says, is simple: The schools in Europe still teach a good deal of geography as a general rule. The schools in the United States do not.

History

The field of history has suffered a similar fate; it has long since been converted into social studies and filled with more social activism and political propaganda than with knowledge of important historic events and persons. In a politically correct educational environment that feeds on anti-American propaganda, it has particularly suffered. Because "social studies" is a rubber term that can mean many things to different persons, school districts and individual schools can often teach whatever they want. And far too often, they do not want to teach American history.

Gross tells the true story of a ten-year-old boy visiting Mount Vernon, Virginia, home of George Washington, with his parents. A *New York Times* reporter asked him if he knew who George Washington was. The boy answered that he "thought" Washington was one of the US presidents. He did not mention that Washington commanded the Revolutionary Army during the War of Independence, that Washington was the nation's *first* president, or that he is often described as "the father of his country." Is it possible that he did not know any of this? Given the lack of American history in the public schools, this is very possible.

Gross reports on the American history curriculum in a well-off Connecticut suburb as well. Up until the fifth grade, the schools there concentrate on studying the community, not the nation or its founding. In the third grade, the children learn the history of their town, starting with the American Indians (Native Americans in today's politically correct terms) and then moving ahead into the present day. In the fourth grade, the schools do not teach any history. In the fifth grade, they provide some training in history. They start with European explorers and show some of the expansion into the vast American West. Gross points out in *The Conspiracy of Ignorance*, "They have still avoided the Founding Fathers, the presidents, the Revolution, and the Civil War"—which, if typical nationally, would explain why half of my college class did not know who James Madison was.

In the sixth grade, students in that Connecticut suburb are taught about "ancient peoples," including the Egyptians, the Eskimos, the people of the Indus Valley in Southeast Asia, and others. Seventh grade history also focuses on earlier times, ending in 1600 and leaving America unmentioned. Finally, in the eighth grade, when the kids are generally thirteen, they get a chance to study the history of their own country: The school district devotes one social studies course to the history of the United States from the colonial period to the present.

Nor do the high schools make up for the lack of education in the earlier grades. Only one course in American history is required to graduate from the high school in that district. Remember, this is a school district in a tony Connecticut suburb, where the schools are generally significantly better than in other parts of the country. If it is this bad in a top suburban high school, there is no reason to believe that urban or rural schools are any better; they are probably worse.

Gross was talking about the teaching of American history some twenty years ago. But I can confirm that the situation today is at best no better, and most likely substantially worse. The college students that I teach, at multiple colleges, again and again show that they know next to nothing about US history. Who wrote the US Constitution? Most do not know. What were Alexander Hamilton's contributions to the founding of the United States? Most do not know. Who was William Tecumseh Sherman? Most do not know. When was Theodore Roosevelt president? Most do not know. When was the Panama Canal built—and by whom? Most do not know. What factors or events drew the United States into World War I? Again, most college students do not know. Most ominously, results from current standardized tests show that as the years go by, American kids know less and less about our nation's history. For example, NAEP test results released in April 2020 showed that *only 15 percent* of eighth graders were at a proficient level or above in US history.

Overwhelmingly, these are good kids. I can attest to that. I teach hundreds every semester. They are honest American kids; they want to live a good life, have a career, experience romantic love and family, have close friends, live a fulfilled and happy life, and so forth. They have been failed by our schools, and their ignorance of the history of their own country is profound—and heartbreaking.

Propaganda

Making matters worse is that the little US "history" that is "taught" is often leftist anti-American propaganda. One example of many is that *A People's History of the United States*, by Howard Zinn, is a popular book in American history courses. Zinn (1922–2010) was a hard-core Marxist and, according to the FBI, an active member of the Communist Party USA (CPUSA) for years. He attended CPUSA meetings in Brooklyn five nights per week and taught a basic Marxism course to other CPUSA members.

Zinn's book is no more than a Communist slur against America. It tells a history of the US in which the United States is almost always wrong. For example, he claims that the United States is not a republic but an empire ruled by a few white men. Christopher Columbus was a genocidal villain. American industrialists and businessmen of the past were exploitative robber barons. Thomas Edison is not mentioned. The scholar Mary Grabar wrote a book titled *Debunking Howard Zinn*. Peter Coclanis, distinguished professor of history at the University of North Carolina at Chapel Hill, says of Zinn's book in a blurb for Grabar's that it is "an execrable work of pseudohistory, full of mistakes, lies, half-truths, and smears." And having read Zinn's book, I can report that Coclanis' brutal assessment is right on target.

And yet, the book is popular among social studies teachers in our high schools and is widely read in American history courses. Grabar's *Debunking Howard Zinn* was published in 2019. In it, she writes: "For years now, teachers have used a variety of editions of *A People's History* with discussion questions, exercises, lesson plans, and activities." She continues: "Many high school students are subjected to Zinn's book in class, along with the America-hating attitude that comes with it." Grabar follows up this claim with true horror stories of student indoctrination with Zinn's ideology. Regarding Zinn's widespread popularity, Grabar cites Gilbert Sewall, director of the American Textbook Council. Sewall pointed out that by 2012, Zinn's book had sold two million copies; Sewall called it the country's "best known work of American history."

A People's History of the United States is pure Marxist propaganda, pushing themes of class warfare and the endless exploitation of the poor by the rich. Historian Harvey Klehr, in a blurb for Grabar's work, noted "the lies, plagiarism, violation of academic standards, and simple-minded platitudes" of Zinn's book. Grabar cites a review by Harvard history professor Oscar Handlin that Zinn's book is a "fairy tale" with "biased selections" that "falsify events."

Zinn ignores, rejects, or denounces everything that makes America special, exceptional, and great. He portrays the American founders as no more than racist supporters of slavery, and capitalism as a system of brutal exploitation. He says the US fought World War II not as a form of self-defense against fascism but merely to make the world safe for the greedy, grasping robber barons who controlled the capitalist system. Finally, he paints the United States as a racist empire that perhaps is little better than Nazi Germany.

Mary Grabar's book refutes the mythology spewed forth by Zinn. She is an immigrant to this country, who was born in Slovenia when it was part of Communist Yugoslavia. Her parents took her and fled from Communism to freedom. She earned a PhD in English from the University of Georgia in 2002, taught at the college level for twenty years, and is a respected researcher at the Alexander Hamilton Institute for the Study of Western Civilization. The title and subtitle of her book on Zinn are telling: *Debunking Howard Zinn: Exposing the Fake History That Turned a Generation Against America.* I have read it. For any parent (or any other responsible citizen) who wants to learn about the anti-American propaganda spewed forth by our schools in many American history courses, Grabar's book is a great place to begin.

Thanks to the combination of too little history education and the teaching of Marxist propaganda, the overwhelming majority of our college students rarely know the following: that the United States was founded on the principle of individual rights; that each individual has an "inalienable right to life, liberty, and the pursuit of happiness"; that this principle led to an abolitionist movement that ended slavery in the US in 1865; that slavery existed all over the world going back into prehistory, and that it still exists in many Communist countries and elsewhere; that American innovators created the electric light, the telephone, the airplane, and much more; that US entrepreneurs and industrialists produced vast amounts of wealth that raised American living standards to unprecedented heights; and that US power and commitment to freedom were indispensable in triumphing over two murderous forms of totalitarianism, National Socialism in World War II and Communism in the Cold War. How about the brutal irony of Zinn and his peers condemning the United States for the slavery it abolished 150 years ago while promoting Communism, a system that continues to employ human slavery in 2022? No, the kids are not taught this.

The fact that my college students repeatedly know little or nothing about American history—or about history in general—frustrates me. It makes my job harder, because I can't draw upon historical examples to illustrate philosophic points—and also, the ignorance of these decent American kids is heartbreaking.

I try to control myself, because if I were to yell, it would sound like I was angry at them; when the truth, of course, is that I am angry at the school system. Yes, it is frustrating for me. But imagine how frustrating it must be to try to live a fulfilled life when you have little reading, writing, or basic math skills, and know little about history or any other academic subject.

Literature

The same sad truth is apparent in the field of literature. Because the schools often abandon the only effective method of teaching reading, the high schools necessarily dumb down the reading lists. For example, in 1922, the Texas state reading list for ninth grade English courses included novels such as Walter Scott's *Ivanhoe* and James Fenimore Cooper's *The Last of the Mohicans*. I have read both of these novels, I have taught literature for years at the high school level, and I use many works of great literature in my college philosophy courses—because outstanding stories *show* serious themes in action; they do not merely *tell* them.

The novels of Scott and Cooper are difficult reading, and perhaps most American college students today would struggle trying to read them; a sizeable minority would not be able to do so. *The estimated grade levels of works on that ninth grade reading list in Texas in 1922 ranged from 8 to 12.9.* The latter is the end-of-senior-year grade level! Contrast this with the Texas ninth grade reading list for 2015–2016. It includes Sandra Cisneros' *The House on Mango Street* and Rodman Philbrick's *Freak the Mighty*. I have not read either of these books, although in fairness, their descriptions on Amazon sound interesting. Nevertheless, the estimated grade levels of the more current list range from 4.5 to 6.7. In the ninth grade! And judging by the weak reading skills of many college students, by what they tell me regarding their high school reading, and by poor reading scores nationwide, this truth about Texas is also true in most other states and most likely all.

Recall that the late Richard Pipes, a history scholar at Harvard University, was saddened by the truth that most applicants for his freshman seminar were unhappily ignorant of the world's great literature. Pipes said, "Our secondary schools are a shambles…. [High school] does not perform its proper function of preparing youth either for citizenship or for higher education."

This sad claim is true in literature and in every other academic subject as well. Nor is the lack of academic training limited to our students. Too often, it also extends to their teachers.

PART TWO

How We Can Fix the
Educational Disaster

CHAPTER TEN

Teacher Training - the Mess That It Is and How We Can Fix It

The year was 1999 and *CliffsNotes* approached me about doing work for them. The company produces a series of study guides that explain many classic novels and other books in brief and simple terms. They hired me to write the study guides for three novels by Ayn Rand: *Anthem*, *The Fountainhead*, and *Atlas Shrugged*. I proceeded to do so. The company's general editor told me in 2000 that when *CliffsNotes* started operation in the late 1950s, their customers were largely high school and college students who wanted help understanding the books they had to read for English class.

In fact, when I was a student in the late 1960s and 1970s, high school English teachers often told us not to read *CliffsNotes*. They acknowledged that the *CliffsNotes* were good—but they did not want us reading the study guides instead of the books. I went on to major in English in college, and the same was true there: The English professors told us to not read *CliffsNotes*.

But by 2000, much had changed. The general editor said that the majority of *CliffsNotes* customers were now high school English teachers. Often they had not read in college the books they were assigned to teach—or worse, had not understood them—and so had to read the study guides to gain an understanding.

Education Instead of Content Courses

How is it possible that many English teachers do not read or do not understand the books that they are assigned to teach? The answer is actually pretty simple.

For if the schools largely neglect academic training, how much knowledge of academic subjects do the teachers need to have? The painful truth is: not much. Teachers-in-training are required to take a number of education courses. Most of them major in education, not in the subject matter they will one day teach. With education as their focus, they necessarily take fewer courses in the subjects that they eventually will teach. In *The Conspiracy of Ignorance*, Martin Gross writes: "Surprisingly, high school teachers are usually less well prepared in the subjects they are going to teach than are ordinary college graduates. High school teachers-in-training typically take fewer credits in their major than other students majoring in the same subject." Put simply, this means that in college, future math teachers take fewer math courses than do math majors, future English teachers take fewer literature courses than do English majors, and so forth. The future teachers take a lot of courses that focus on how to teach rather than on what to teach.

Gross uses Connecticut, a state that takes pride in its "excellent" school system, as an example. Twenty years ago, at the University of Connecticut, in order to receive a Bachelor of Science (B.S.) degree in mathematics, a candidate must have completed forty hours of training in math and an additional twelve in related sciences, such as physics and chemistry. By contrast, to become certified to teach math in the Connecticut public high schools, a candidate needed to complete only thirty hours of math training and nine hours in other sciences. This means that a nonteaching math major must take 25 percent more courses in math and science (thirteen out of fifty-two) than a high school math teacher. Has the situation improved at all in recent years? It has not. Today, a high school math teacher in Connecticut is still required to take only thirty credit hours of mathematics, while students are required to take forty credit hours of math to graduate with a math degree from the University of Connecticut.

If possible, the training for elementary school teachers in content courses such as math or science is even worse. The college students preparing for teaching at this level also major in education. Studies show that for them, education courses make up a solid 40 percent of their course work—or roughly fifty credits of the 120 they are required to take. Gross points out that this means they take only seventy credits of content courses, making their degrees little more educational than those gained from two-year colleges.

Without a doubt, there are still dedicated, experienced, competent teachers in the public school system. Nevertheless, the general truth about American public school teachers is grim. In his book, *Inside American Education*, the brilliant scholar Thomas Sowell wrote in 1993:

> *Consistently, for decades, those college students who have majored in education have been among the least qualified of all college students.... Whether measured by Scholastic Aptitude Tests, ACT tests, vocabulary tests, reading comprehension tests, or Graduate Record Examinations, students majoring in education have consistently scored below the national average.... In short, educators are drawing disproportionately from the dregs of the college-educated population.*

Twenty years later, Richard Vedder, an economist at Ohio University, wrote an essay titled "The Alarming Truth About Education Majors" in *The Fiscal Times* regarding US teacher training. He cited evidence from a study done by the National Council on Teacher Quality (NCTQ). Among the council's findings: The nations whose students outperform American kids recruit teachers-in-training from the top third of college students; whereas in the US only 25 percent of education programs restrict admission to even the top half of college students. This means that 75 percent of US education schools accept applicants from the bottom half of college students.

Regarding what the education schools teach their students, the NCTQ study found: "Only 11 percent of elementary programs and 47 percent of secondary programs are providing adequate content preparation in the subjects they will teach." Vedder comments on these NCTQ findings, "This comports with what I have observed. The students majoring in education are below average academically, with relatively low test scores and high school rank. They often have so-so preparation in the subject matters they are going to teach."

We can conclude two things about most US public school teachers: First, those who major in education are generally academically weaker than college students pursuing other majors. Second, as already seen, education majors take fewer content courses than do most other college kids. They come into college academically weaker than most college students, and upon graduation, the gap has widened. And these are the people who will teach academic content to our children.

Knowing what we have so far discussed in this book, the only point surprising about my *CliffsNotes* story is that the teachers are occasionally assigned challenging books to teach.

Teacher Training Must Focus on Content

Teacher training is just one area where many foreign nations focus on academics more than the United States. In Germany, for example, teachers-in-training are required to be significantly stronger academically than their US counterparts. An essay titled "Germany is Desperate for Teachers" at the website DW Made for Minds describes the high academic standards expected of teachers in Germany: "The traditional route to become a teacher is demanding. High school graduates must show near-perfect grades in numerous subjects to be accepted to universities' teach-er-training programs, which take seven to eight years." Gross writes in *The Conspiracy of Ignorance* that German teacher candidates must first "get an undergraduate degree in a *content subject.* Only then can they take graduate work in education to prepare for the classroom."

Knowing methods of teaching is useless if you do not know the content to teach.

Because public school teachers are expected to know little content, teacher certification tests in most states are pitched at about a tenth-grade level. What happened in Massachusetts in the late 1990s when the degree of diffi-culty on such tests was raised? The results were hair-raising. Eighteen hundred aspiring teachers took the initial test in the spring of 1998. Overwhelmingly, these were candidates who had graduated from a four-year college with a degree in education. The test was divided into three segments: reading, writing, and the subject area in which the wannabe instructor would teach. The results were a disaster. *Fifty-nine percent of the aspiring teachers flunked the exam.* And while the degree of intellectual difficulty had been raised, the starting bar was very low.

When the test was given again several months later to 2,100 applicants, the results were slightly less bad: Only 47 percent of the education graduates failed. The state of Massa-chusetts permitted applicants to take the test as many times as they liked. Still, wannabe teachers were failing on the second and third try. Why? The test was now pitched at an advanced high school or early college level. Why were college gradu-ates, and those supposedly prepared to be *teachers*, failing by the hundreds? By this point, the answer is obvious: because schools of education do not prepare future teachers effectively in reading, writing, math, or the subjects they will one day teach. Recent years have seen little progress: In Massachusetts, some 48 percent of aspiring teachers still fail the mathematics certifying exam the first time they take it.

There are other horror stories related to teacher training. Arthur Bestor was an American professor of history at several colleges. In 1953, he wrote a book on the poor state of US education, titled *Educational Wastelands*. In it, he told the true story of a top English student who was discouraged from pursuing the teaching career she was seeking *because her grades were too high!* The student says a professor of education "told me that prospective teachers of English who had straight-A averages…were very apt to become scholars rather than good teachers, concerned only with academic research." She assured him she very much wanted to be a teacher. He responded that her love of the subject matter meant she likely would bury herself in her books rather than work with the students. As she relates it, "Emphasis on subject matter and knowledge of it, he implied, were outdated, because 'we don't teach subject matter, we teach children.'"

They teach children…what? Obviously not math, literature, science, or history. Bestor pointed out the takeaway of this and similar stories: The American schools of education have so completely rejected academic subjects as the proper content of education that to them, a teaching candidate's mastery of his or her field is a problem, not a benefit. It is a "failing" that can disqualify a candidate from a teaching career.

Think of the insanity of this and imagine, for a moment, if it were true in other fields. Suppose a college student excels in a biology major, wants to go to medical school and become a doctor, is a straight A-student, is top of the class, and aces the medical school entrance exams. But the medical schools turn down the student because, they say, that love of biology and medicine means the student likely will spend more time with test tubes in the lab than with patients. The student assures them of wanting to be a doctor and help cure patients, rather than being a researcher, but they are suspicious of the ability in and love of the subject, and prefer a lesser candidate.

How many of us would want to go to—or bring our kids to—the lesser medical student rather than the outstanding one? That's right, nobody. If this rejection of subject matter filled our schools of medicine the way it fills our schools of education, the result would be a terrible decline in the quality of medical care—just as it has resulted in a terrible decline in the quality of schooling.

Doctors are trusted with our children's bodies; teachers are trusted with their minds. It is just as important to have the best teachers educating our kids' minds as it is to have the best doctors treating their bodies.

Notice that numerous examples in this chapter are decades old. It is fair to ask if the situation has improved in recent years. The proof is in the pudding—in this case, in the kids' mastery of academic subjects, as demonstrated on standardized tests both national and international. *And academic test scores keep going down.* At best, they are stagnant.

How to Train Teachers

I have heard people say in defense of teaching method rather than content, "We all know people who understand a subject well but who cannot explain it. They do not know how to teach. So it is good for them to study a lot of teaching method." I understand this objection, but I do not agree. People who really know a subject—who *really* know it—can explain it well. In fact, they are the only ones who can. This raises the question, What does it mean to really know a subject?

The answer is to know it from the ground up, to grasp its concepts in terms of the many examples these concepts refer to, to "see it like a truck," as one of my philosophy professors said. As one example, suppose a history teacher is teaching a high school class on the Cold War. Such a course would involve explaining the difference between the two main enemies, the USA and the USSR. A good teacher would explain the differences between freedom and dictatorship; between individual rights on the one hand and a totalitarian state on the other. He or she would start with a flood of examples. Freedom and individual rights, the teacher would point out, mean that you, John Doe or Katie Simmons or whomever, get to choose what type of work you will do in your career; that you get to choose where you want to live; that you are free to travel and to leave the country; that you can speak out against government policy; that you can hold and express religious views or not; that writers can write the books they want; that singers can sing the songs they want; that filmmakers can make the films they want; and that you can choose to read, listen to, or watch their work—or not.

An effective teacher would then explain how this contrasts with life in a dictatorship: The government might decide the work you do in your career; the government must give permission for you to live in a given area; you are not free to travel even within the country without government permission, and you certainly cannot leave the country; if you speak out against the government, you will be arrested by the secret police; if under the Communists you openly hold religious views, you might be imprisoned and condemned to slave labor; artists cannot choose the books, songs, or films they will create—only those works approved by the government can be created, and those are the only ones that you as a fan are permitted to enjoy.

This is effective teaching. Such a flood of examples takes political concepts that are often fuzzy in people's minds and makes them real. It shows what they mean in practice, in the real world. In this particular example, it shows what the contrasting systems of freedom and dictatorship look like in action. An ability to do this is one aspect of *really knowing* a subject. It means that you hold in your mind the ideas or concepts of a subject in terms of the many instances or illustrations to which they refer in our world.

We must train our teachers to know their subject from the ground up, to "see it like a truck," to illustrate the subject's theories and principles with a flood of examples that tie those theories and principles to reality. This is one trait of an outstanding teacher.

One effective way to tie ideas to the everyday world is to tell stories. The stories can be real or fictional; their purpose is to show what the ideas being taught look like or lead to in human life. Stories, especially powerful ones, bring ideas to life! Here is an example: One day in class, we discussed the aging process, its difficulties and its benefits…. Wait…what? the kids said. There are benefits to getting old? There sure are, I said. What? they asked. I'll tell you a true story, I said.

"It was the first year I taught at Kingston College [not the school's real name]. One student was in the hospital, and she died from a rare form of meningitis. Another student was on her way back to school after Thanksgiving break. She collided with a semi on the interstate and was killed instantly. A third student, a kid on the football team, got into a barroom brawl in town and was stabbed to death. Not one of these kids was older than twenty-one. If someone lives a long life; has a fulfilling career, an enduring romantic relationship, and a loving relationship with his or her children; and dies in his or her eighties after a long, rich life, this is a sad but not tragic event. But when a person dies at age twenty-one, with what should be an entire life ahead, this is a tragedy. One great virtue, although not the only one, of aging is that we did not die young; we had a shot at a long and enriched life."

The students nodded. They were saddened by this story, as the students in every class are when I tell it—but their very sadness shows their understanding of the point.

Good teachers tell stories. They command the students' attention with a tale that is: 1. dramatic and fascinating, and 2. relevant to the theme or the idea to be taught.

Let me relate a very different story, illustrating a much happier truth, also from class discussion. One day, we were discussing the power of romantic love. A great love story occurred to me, and I asked them if they knew the true story of Robert Browning and Elizabeth Barrett. Who? they asked. They had never heard of these two. So I told them.

"The time period is the 1840s. The place is London. Elizabeth Barrett was a famed poetess but was bedridden with illness. She had weak lungs, was in her late thirties, and was not expected to live much longer. Robert Browning was a young man, a dynamic and brilliant poet, largely unappreciated by the literary crowd but admired by Elizabeth. He fell in love with her through her poetry, he wrote to her, they corresponded back and forth, he came to visit her, and they clicked. He proposed to her. But her father was an overbearing tyrant toward his children. He refused to let any of them marry and was especially jealous about Elizabeth, his firstborn and favorite. But the love she and Robert shared made her stronger both in bodily health and in spirit. She agreed to marry him. They eloped, they escaped, they left London and England altogether, and they moved to sunny, warmer Italy. Elizabeth had an olive Mediterranean complexion—dark hair and dark eyes, looking like she hailed from Southern Europe rather than England—so Robert's pet name for her was 'my little Portuguese.'

"The woman people feared would not survive another winter lived fifteen more years, shared a deep love with her husband, gave birth to a healthy child, and wrote beautiful love poetry, including a slim volume dedicated to the man she loved. She titled it 'Sonnets from the Portuguese,' which contains one of the most famous poems ever composed, beginning with the immortal lines 'How do I love thee?

Let me count the ways.' After many years together, she died in her husband's arms. Robert lived another twenty-eight years. He battled intense grief over Elizabeth's death and never remarried, but he developed into one of Britain's leading nineteenth-century poets. Their relationship is perhaps the most beautiful real-life love story I know, and one that forcefully illustrates the power of romantic love to transform a person's life."

The students were riveted by this story. I then led them into a deeper discussion: What is the meaning of romantic love in human life? Is it tied to the personal values of each lover? For example, Robert and Elizabeth shared a love of poetry and literature. Is this an integral component of love? And what about cherished values that are distinctly personal and not dependent on another person? For example, Robert mourned Elizabeth deeply and never remarried—but he developed into a superb poet. Such individualized goals and loves are part of a person's own soul, and they cannot be taken away. What role do such personal values play in romantic love and in a fulfilled life more broadly? A good teacher will start with a specific, targeted story and then lead class discussion into deep and important issues. And the more difficult the material, the greater the need becomes for vivid stories to illustrate it.

Philosophy is a challenging subject that seeks to answer life's broadest and deepest questions: What is human nature? What kind of a world do we inhabit? What is the good? What is the good society? How do we know? To make the subjects clear for my students, I introduce stories into our discussions.

Let us say my class is discussing the issues of political philosophy. The main question of the field can be expressed in differing forms. What is the good society? What is the proper relationship between an individual and the state? What is the best form of government? What type of economic system is best suited to human beings? In the course of discussing such questions, we always study the works of two famous English political philosophers, Thomas Hobbes and John Locke. (Locke, of course, had a great influence on the American Revolution.) Hobbes thought human beings were irrational brutes who needed law and order rammed down their throats by a powerful police state. Locke, by contrast, thought human beings were generally rational beings, willing to work honestly and therefore capable of self-governing. They needed no political strongman to force them to live in a civilized way. They could live peacefully and productively under freedom.

"Let's do a thought experiment," I say to the students. "In our imaginations, let's travel to the most crime-ridden country, city, or neighborhood we can think of. Once there, who or what does Hobbes see? He sees the drug dealers, getting rich on people's misery and addictions. He sees the muggers, knocking down old ladies and stealing their purses. He sees the heist artists, sticking up a gas station or a liquor store at gunpoint. And that's all he sees. Locke, on the other hand, sees the criminals—but he sees the honest people as well, the victims on whom the criminals prey. He sees the worker running for the train or bus to get to work on time. He sees the mother pushing her child in a stroller to a grocery store to buy a quart of milk. He sees the merchants unlocking their stores and preparing to sell goods to their customers. Locke sees a much wider scope of human beings than does Hobbes."

This thought experiment serves to illustrate an important principle about human life: For two reasons, Hobbes is mistaken in thinking that human beings are generally irrational brutes. First, it is obviously false. We all know people, probably many, who are sane, rational, kind, and generous. Second, it is logically impossible—because brutes or criminals require victims. Thugs do not create wealth. They don't grow food, ship it to market, or sell it in stores. They don't invent or repair cars, or produce or sell gasoline for them. They don't drive the crosstown bus or study medicine and become doctors; they don't invent cell phones, CD players, personal computers, or software—and so on. They rely upon honest working people to do these things, and then they steal from the honest people. Criminals are parasites. A society of them would soon die from mass starvation. My thought experiment is a good story illustrating these truths about politics. This is the kind of method employed by effective teachers to relate a subject to their students.

Another aspect of truly and deeply understanding a field is the ability to give exact definitions of its key ideas. To return to the freedom-versus-dictatorship example discussed above: "Individual rights" means that your life belongs to you, not to the state. It means that an individual has an "inalienable right to life, liberty, and the pursuit of happiness." This is the essence of the principle. To explain it further, it means that you have all the rights noted previously. Above all, it means that the proper job of a government is to protect those rights. Similarly, "freedom" means the ability to live your life as you choose in the absence of physical force initiated against you, whether by private criminals or the government.

By contrast, "dictatorship" means that your life belongs not to you but to the state. To explain further: The government has the legal authority and physical power to force you to do whatever it wants, and can severely punish you if you do not obey: It can imprison, enslave, torture, or murder you. If you are lucky, it will merely exile you. A totalitarian state, as the name implies, holds total life-and-death power over its citizens. It closes the borders with walls and machine gun outposts, so that people can't get out. In its Communist version, it brainwashes kids in school to love Communism and to hate the free countries of the world. It wipes out freedom of speech and religion, and harshly punishes those who disobey. It even requires citizens to get an internal passport in order to travel within the country. It is the total state, controlling every aspect of its citizens' lives.

Examples, stories, definitions—these are a few aspects of really knowing a subject. There are others, but these three make a great start. One who knows a subject well enough to provide these will be a great communicator and has the right stuff to be an outstanding teacher. *We must train our teachers to know their subjects super well.*

I am considered a very good teacher, and have Teacher of the Year awards from two colleges. If I were hired to do teacher training with future teachers who really know their subject, *I could do it effectively in one course—it does not take fifty credits of college education.*

In no particular order, here are a few things I would teach them. I would teach them to stay in motion, because this creates more energy. I would teach them to move around the classroom; to get relatively close to all the students so they could watch them more carefully; to monitor them during class discussion. I would teach them to change the pitch of their voice, to avoid a droning monotone. I would teach them to yell at times, not in anger but in excitement, to create enthusiasm. I would teach them to write material on the board, so the students' motor skills, as well as their eyes and ears, are involved in the learning process as they take notes. I would teach them to stand sideways at the board, their head turned to face the students, so as they write, they can both watch the kids and be heard by them. I would emphasize that a good teacher both loves the subject matter and cares about the kids. The first enables the teacher to generate enthusiasm; the second drives him or her to do everything possible to advance the kids' education. I would teach them to ask a question at the start of class on a topic they want to discuss, to take five to ten minutes to allow the students to write a brief answer, and then to begin the discussion. This gives the kids time to think about it and prepare, and it provides them with something right in front of them to refer to. Regarding homework, I would teach them to have the kids do a written summary of all readings, to collect these, and to check them. This is to ensure that the students do the reading. There are many other things I would teach future teachers, but these few give an indication of how to do it.

There is one other aspect of teacher training that is important—to work with outstanding teachers who have a substantial amount of classroom experience. In our fictional example, as part of their single course in teacher training, I would have future teachers observe me (or some other veteran teacher) repeatedly in the classroom and discuss my methods with me. I would have them teach sample classes, to be critiqued by me or some other master teacher. Early in the semester, the budding teacher would observe me; later in the semester, the positions would be reversed and I would observe and critique the sample classes. This classroom time is especially important for elementary school teachers, because for them classroom management is critically important. A group of little kids together in a class is a lot to handle, and a budding teacher needs many hours in the classroom with an experienced elementary teacher to master this skill.

Above all, I would urge the aspiring teachers: "Give lots of examples! Tell vivid stories! Tie the ideas to the real world! Define key terms! Write the definitions on the board! Make sure the students copy down the definitions of the most important ideas! Above all, give lots of examples; tell stories, whether real or fictional; tie the ideas to reality and bring them to life!

Know the content! That's the first requirement to be a superb teacher.

CHAPTER ELEVEN

The Impregnable Fortress

Terry McAuliffe, former governor of Virginia, recently ignited a controversy when he said that parents should not tell schools what to teach their children. Indeed, in numerous cases around the country, parents openly disagree with the policies of their local schools only to be labeled "domestic terrorists" by the National School Board Association and the Department of Justice. A school superintendent in Arizona has recently been accused of hiring a private investigator to dig up information on dissenting parents. McAuliffe and the others claim that parents should have little or no say regarding what the schools teach their children. In the field of education, this is currently an all-too-common belief.

Who Holds the Power in US Schools?

The painful struggle of parents to have a voice in the education of their children shows how little authority they currently hold. Who does hold the power in American schooling? Who is responsible for the disaster it has become?

And, whoever those people are, is it possible to change their minds and their policies? In order to fix the mess that US education has become, we need answers to these questions.

In the previous chapter, we briefly discussed points about teacher training made by Arthur Bestor. He made deeper points, as well. In his book, *Educational Wastelands*, he talked about the schools of education, the federal and state departments of education, and the "superintendents, principals, and other local public school administrators and supervisors." Bestor says that these people hold the power in US schooling. They are responsible for how we got into this mess, why the problem has lasted so long, why the schools make no positive changes, and why schooling continues to get worse. Bestor calls this group an "interlocking directorate."

The dictionary defines "directorate" as "a body of directors"—those who hold power over an organization or group of other people. "Interlocking," of course, refers to parts that lock in with one another—or fit together.

Bestor is absolutely right. These individuals and organizations do form an interlocking directorate of schooling in the United States. They have held the power for a century, they still hold it, and they are responsible for the disaster that is American schooling.

If US public schooling is to improve, the interlocking directorate must change its policies regarding its approach to education. Is it open to change? That is the all-important question. In order to answer it, let's take a deeper dive into the people who comprise this directorate, and what they think.

E.D. Hirsch was a professor of humanities at the University of Virginia. In 1996, his well-known book *The*

Schools We Need and Why We Don't Have Them was published. Hirsch, like Bestor decades earlier, critically examined the interlocking directorate. He points out its utter refusal to change educational principles and policies. By the 1990s, it had long rejected academic subjects as the proper content of teaching, which Hirsch points out; and it continues to do so today, in the 2020s. Hirsch, knowing how to communicate his points, tells stories, in this case true ones.

The Bias Against Facts

He spoke at meetings of professional educators, generally attended by several hundred principals and school administrators from across the nation. At one of these meetings, someone asked Hirsch what sorts of things first graders should know. In *The Schools We Need and Why We Don't Have Them*, he writes of his reply: "some elements of geography, like being able to find North, South, East, and West both out of doors and on globes and maps, as well as being able to identify both the Atlantic and Pacific Oceans and the seven continents." The educators disagreed. One asked if Hirsch truly thought it helped a first grader to know Earth's continents. Either no one at the meeting agreed with Hirsch, or no one had the courage to speak up in defense of factual knowledge.

In reality, of course it benefits a kid to know the facts of geography. There are basics of knowledge that serve as building blocks of higher knowledge. For example, we should study reading in the early grades using superb children's books (and systematic phonics), and gradually, over the years, build to more and more advanced books and stories. We should master arithmetic while young, and then build on it to learn algebra, geometry, and trig. Just so, knowledge of continents and oceans is a base for people to advance to knowing the countries of the world, the major rivers and mountains, the states of our country, the state capitals, and so on. This is the start of growing into a knowledgeable person. If subjects are well taught by knowledgeable teachers, it is not that difficult for a motivated kid to learn a great deal.

It is really not that hard to rise up out of ignorance. ("Ignorant," of course, means lacking knowledge, not lacking intelligence.)

In the same book, Hirsch discusses another meeting of educators, in which he pointed out the joy of learning "the relations between the earth and the sun during a year's orbit, and why, at the equator, spring and fall are the hottest seasons." Again, the professional educators—members of the "interlocking directorate"—disagreed. One asked if such knowledge made a student "a better person."

If it were me, I would have replied, "Does ignorance make someone a better person?" The honest answer to both questions is no. Being a better person means being honest, responsible, trustworthy, and kind. It is a *moral issue*, an issue of character. Neither gaining knowledge nor failing to gain it will make someone a better person. There are people who are both knowledgeable and good, and those who are knowledgeable and not so good. Just so, there are those who are ignorant and good, and some who are ignorant and not so good. Being knowledgeable rather than ignorant will make someone *a more effective person, not a morally better one.* Knowledge gives us the ability to better understand the world and the people in it, and so, to deal with the world and relate to the people in more positive and beneficial ways.

One striking example is knowledge of American history, especially of its founding—understanding the ideas of Thomas Jefferson, James Madison, and the other founders, ideas expressed in the Declaration of Independence, the United States Constitution, and the Bill of Rights. As we saw earlier, too often US history is not taught in the American schools. It is a tragedy, because such knowledge would drive home to us the things that make this country special and great, the reasons that millions of immigrants struggled to get here, why millions more still seek to immigrate here, and why it is proper and right that they do so.

Above all, what American children need to learn is the moral principle that makes America the greatest nation of history: the principle of individual rights, that your life belongs to you, not to the state or the church. The American people—you, I, any of us—would be much more informed citizens then, better able to understand political issues, to judge between parties and candidates, to grasp both domestic and international issues at a deeper level, and to make more informed choices in the voting booth. In our lives, such knowledge would benefit us in our roles as citizens, would enable us to participate more effectively in the democratic process, and would make the United States a nation of stronger, more knowledgeable people.

Morality Based Upon Earlier Knowledge

But does having factual knowledge make someone a better person?

Yes, in a deeper sense, there is a way in which it does. Suppose, for example, that children's schooling does provide them a substantial amount of knowledge—that they are good readers, can write an effective essay, know a good amount of history, and have read and studied great literature in high school. They are prepared for and enroll in college and, let us say, study philosophy in one of my courses. *We will read and discuss in depth a great deal of moral philosophy!* We will take a deep dive into questions such as, What is human nature? What does it mean for a human being to be a good person? What is justice? Should I act in my own self-interest, should I sacrifice for others, or is there a balance of the two? We will examine the most important moral questions of human life—and yes, such knowledge can make someone a better person.

Some people believe that it is morally right to sacrifice ourselves for other people, especially if those people are important in our lives. Call this the self-sacrifice school of ethics. Others believe that it is morally right for a person to love good things and persons—an education, a career in a cherished field, an honest man or woman, one's children—and to pursue these goals and relationships, to fulfill them, and never to sacrifice them. Call this the self-fulfillment school of ethics. In class, I point out to the students that in many cultures, arranged marriages are still popular. The parents of a boy agree with the parents of a girl that when the children are old enough, they will marry. If the boy or girl says, "But I don't love him (or her)," the response is, "You do this for your parents. It is your moral duty to sacrifice for your family." On the other hand, in the United States and many other nations, people generally marry for love. They love each other, they expect to be happy with each other for the rest of their lives, and they expect their family to honor and respect their choice of spouse. They fulfill themselves, they do not sacrifice, and they expect the important people in their lives to give their blessing.

What is the right approach? Pursue one's own loves and values, or surrender them to satisfy the demands of other people? The two schools of ethics apply to issues other than marriage. But this is one good example of the moral question. We discuss it deeply and at length in class. At the end of the day, each individual must make his or her own choice on such a personal issue. But we study and think carefully about these issues. Does an individual have the right to his or her own life and to pursue personal happiness, as Thomas Jefferson wrote in the Declaration of Independence? Or should other people's wants count more than an individual's own values and loves? Is it "selfish" to pursue what I want in disregard of my family and society? On the other hand, is it mean-spirited and authoritarian to demand people to sacrifice their values? Thinking honestly about such important questions and others greatly increases our moral understanding and *helps us take moral issues seriously*. This will definitely make us better persons.

But you cannot understand higher mathematics, such as calculus, without first mastering arithmetic and algebra. Similarly, you cannot understand the difficult issues of moral philosophy without a solid grounding in reading, writing, history, literature, and other basics of the humanities. Knowledge builds in steps, and moral philosophy, near the top of the pyramid, can help us become better persons.

Hirsch points out that the interlocking directorate holds an endless bias against factual learning. In *The Schools We Need*, Hirsch discusses the repeated instances of an anti-fact bias he encountered among professional educators. He writes: "I encountered similar attitudes regarding the uselessness of factual knowledge and the undesirability of asking students to learn it." The members of the interlocking directorate said that they supported "true knowledge" as distinct from "mere facts." Hirsch asked them to define what they meant by "true knowledge," and they replied that it means "knowing the interrelations of things." Hirsch pointed out: "[But] they did not explain how things can be related without first being known."

Let's bring in a few examples of why Hirsch is right. Looking at a house cat and a lion, it is not obvious that they are part of the same animal family. After all, a full-grown male lion weighs some four hundred pounds and towers over a ten- or twelve-pound house cat. But they are part of the same family—a lion is a type of cat. How in the world could anyone know the relationship between lions and other types of cats without first knowing house cats and lions? No one could. Facts about different kinds of cats must be known first in order to understand the relationships between and among them.

Similarly, the Appalachian Mountains in the eastern United States are not very high; some of them reach perhaps four to six thousand feet in elevation. The Himalayan Mountains in Asia are the tallest peaks in the world. Mount

Everest, for example, in Nepal, stands some twenty-nine thousand feet above sea level. But millions of years ago, the Appalachians were as tall or taller than the Himalayas! In part, erosion wore them down…and, over millions of years, will help wear down the Himalayas, too. Again, we could not know the comparisons of or relationships between different mountain ranges if we did not first know about the mountain ranges themselves. Hirsch is right: Facts are the necessary building blocks of more advanced knowledge.

Proving the Truth of a Claim Requires Factual Evidence

I have taught logic for forty years. Once in class, I stated a point I thought was true. A student immediately responded, "That's your opinion." I thought about it for several moments, and then I asked, "Is everything an opinion? How do we distinguish something as true from a mere opinion or belief?" The students thought for a while, and then one of them said, "You back it up." I nodded. "Correct," I said, "but back it up with what?" The kid said, "With facts." Again, I nodded. "Exactly correct."

To show that some belief or conclusion is true, we must support it with factual evidence. The whole point of logic as a field is to teach us how to provide evidence; what is relevant to a conclusion and what is not; and how much evidence is necessary to prove a conclusion.

Let me provide another example. I believe that global warming (or climate change) is overwhelmingly natural, and only trivially manmade, and I have published two essays on the topic. Rational human beings can disagree honestly on this, and on many other points as well. But no matter where we stand on this controversial issue, we need to provide evidence to support our beliefs. So what is my evidence? In no particular order: There have been ice ages in Earth's past in which the temperatures dropped a great deal and the ice advanced; then, in time, the temperatures rose and the ice melted. The temperature swings were much greater than what we experience today.

Some of these ice ages occurred millions of years before man's earliest ancestors appeared on Earth. What caused them? The complex relationship between the earth and the sun. In other words, the power of nature is awesome. Also, those who believe in manmade warming claim that carbon dioxide buildup in the atmosphere causes a "greenhouse effect," trapping heat and raising temperatures, which, in so far as it goes, is true. Nevertheless, there was a time in Earth's distant past when *CO2 buildup in the atmosphere was ten times what it is today, yet the earth was in the depths of an ice age.* This tells us that although carbon dioxide buildup in the atmosphere is a factor in warming, it is a weaker one that can be, and at times is, overwhelmed by stronger ones.

Roy Spencer provides more evidence. Spencer holds a PhD in meteorology from the University of Wisconsin and, with his partner, John Christie, pioneered NASA's satellite program to measure Earth's temperatures, which give us the most accurate temperature readings available of Earth's atmosphere. Spencer claims that 95 percent of carbon dioxide spewed each year into the atmosphere comes from natural sources, not manmade ones. Tim Ball, a veteran Canadian climate scientist, says the amount is

96 percent. One source is the oceans, which contain fifty times as much carbon dioxide as the atmosphere. Habibullo Abdussamatov, born in Uzbekistan, is a Russian astrophysicist and a leader in studying the connection between the sun and the earth's climate. He reminds us: When the sun is at the high point of the sunspot cycle, it releases more radiation; more heat thereby reaches the earth's surface, warming the oceans, which, via evaporation, causes enormous amounts of carbon dioxide to be released into the atmosphere. Abdussamatov and numerous other scientists point out that carbon dioxide buildup in the atmosphere is a *result, not a cause* of warming. Not surprisingly, during the twentieth century, the sun was at a high point in its cycle of emitting radiation.

Is this enough evidence to prove that global warming is natural, and not manmade? No, but it's a good start. This example shows how to go about changing an opinion into truth: You support a belief with a wealth of facts. People who know few facts, whose education did not include the teaching of many facts, may hold opinions—but without the knowledge to back them up. We all have probably known such opinionated people in our lives, loud in voicing a belief but slow in providing supporting facts. They're annoying, to put it mildly, and do not help us arrive at truth in any field. Facts are a critical building block of knowledge.

Today, members of the interlocking directorate hold the same antifact attitude as did those with whom Hirsch spoke some twenty-five years ago, the same attitude they have held for a century. Their belief that facts are useless to a child's education would be comical were it not so harmful to the kids. These same "educators" are unwilling to admit that their anti-fact approach is related to the terrible test scores that American students repeatedly get. (Talk about a need to understand the "interrelations of things!")

In *The Schools We Need*, Hirsch writes in frustration: "There was no sense of a connection between [the] educator's own antiknowledge attitudes and the current academic incompetence of our students as measured by world standards. There was no thought of a possible causal relation between lack of factual knowledge and lack of ability to read, write, and solve math problems." These "educators" are deeply out of touch with what a good education really is.

The Interlocking Directorate Runs a Vast Near Monopoly

Both Arthur Bestor and E.D. Hirsch pointed out a series of sad truths about members of the interlocking directorate. The members raise few or no objections from within about their policies; they continue to support the same ideas, in new dress and with new names, that have caused the disaster our schools have become; they close ranks and uniformly reject criticisms from outside their circle; they are extremely unwilling to submit their educational policies to parents and to the public for open discussion and debate; and, perhaps worst of all, they engage in smears, verbal abuse, and name-calling of outside critics, no matter how qualified, insightful, and well-informed those critics are. Today, members of the interlocking directorate are the spiritual descendants of professors at Columbia University's Teachers College going back a century to the days of William Heard Kilpatrick and John Dewey (in Columbia's philosophy department).

They support the same antiacademic approach to education, and they shower critics who oppose them with the same kind of insults. For example, recently the National School Board Association—a charter member of the interlocking directorate—smeared as "domestic terrorists" parents who oppose the teaching of critical race theory to their children. Other charter members of the interlocking directorate have denounced people who support phonics as members of the political far right. Presumably, they will either ignore this book or dismiss it as the know-nothing ramblings of an ignoramus regarding the field of education.

Recall from earlier in the book that in 1983, a commission appointed by President Ronald Reagan's secretary of education published its findings about US schooling in a piece titled "A Nation at Risk." This report concluded that US schooling was so bad that "if an unfriendly foreign power had attempted to impose on America the mediocre educational performance that exists today, we might well have viewed it as an act of war." This is the strongest possible language and came from a commission appointed by a cabinet-level official. But has anything in US schooling improved in the thirty-nine years since? No. In fact, it has gotten worse.

In the United States, the interlocking directorate runs a vast near monopoly: Some 89 percent of American students ages five to seventeen go to the public schools. The kids are forced to go there by compulsory attendance laws, and the schools are funded by money that taxpayers are forced to give. The interlocking directorate gets victims (students) and money by force. In fact, very often the public schools *get more money because they are failing.* This is one reason the interlocking directorate pays no attention to criticisms that its schools are terrible.

Hirsch is right: The interlocking directorate, in our day and for many years in the past, is and has been an impregnable fortress. Its members hold power over American schooling, they will not change their harmful policies, and nobody—not the secretary of education, not the president of the United States, not the US Congress, not anybody else—can convince or force them to improve their methods. Visionary entrepreneur Elon Musk, whose company SpaceX is determined to land men on Mars within several decades, says: "It is easier to land a man on Mars than to change the schooling system…" Musk is exactly right—and we have seen the reasons why.

At the start of this chapter, I raised the question of whether the powers that be in US schooling will change their disastrous anti-education policies. We have seen that the answer is a resounding no. The interlocking directorate is exactly how Hirsch terms it in *The Schools We Need*: an "impregnable fortress." In brief, the interlocking directorate is a fortress that cannot be overrun, conquered, or reformed.

But it can be outflanked.

CHAPTER TWELVE

Parents in Charge - the Past

Laura Kronen is a homeschooling mom of two boys in Georgia. Her sons are doing very well. She tells us the reasons that homeschooling is becoming a popular option for many families. There are often bullies and thugs in the public schools that make a child's physical safety a concern. Today, the schools indoctrinate kids with endless leftist propaganda regarding dangerous manmade global warming, critical race theory, the evils of America, the need to replace capitalism with socialism, and much more. Above all, there are the terrible academics. Kronen shares that homeschooled students generally score higher on standardized academic tests than do public school students. For example, homeschooled kids generally score seventy-two points higher on the SATs than the national average; and on the ACT, for which the national average is twenty-one points out of thirty-six, homeschooled kids' average is 22.8. This is just one example of many that shows the excellent results of parents controlling the education of their children.

Who should hold the final authority in education? The question is easy to answer: parents. This is especially true when part of the interlocking directorate is made up of powerful government agencies. These agencies, and the directorate as a whole, are unaccountable to the people for whom they should be working: the parents of the students. Why is this so? For two reasons: First is that the schools get money and students by force, and so have no economic incentive to change. Second is that the interlocking directorate holds an explicit anti-intellectual "educational" philosophy and so is not abashed by the academic ignorance of many US students. The directorate reports to nobody. It is, truly, an impregnable fortress. It cannot and will not be changed.

But with enough dedication, we can circumvent it. Let's begin with a historical truth to introduce this important point.

Andrew Coulson (1967–2016) was an educational researcher who wrote a book titled *Market Education*. In it, he examined the history of education, contrasting results of societies in which parents controlled schooling with outcomes of societies in which the government controlled schooling. It is not surprising that results in the former are almost always better than in the latter.

There are several simple reasons for this. One is that in a large majority of cases, Mom and Dad love Junior more than the government does. A second is that Mom and Dad almost always know Junior's needs and interests better than the government can. Loving parents, in discussion with the child, should have the final say regarding the curriculum taught to the child. And we know the curriculum that parents overwhelmingly want for their children: They want the kids to read effectively, which means the use of systematic phonics. They want their children to write well and, in time, to write college-level essays. They want the kids to master arithmetic and then move on to higher mathematics. Parents want their children to study history—not a weird hybrid called social studies—and in the United States want them to know American history, including an unbiased account of the nation's founding period. They want the schools to teach the basics of science to the students, and to teach them great literature.

They want the kids to pursue an academic program, perhaps with courses teaching practical skills and vocational training as options in the later years of high school; but they want their kids to have solid thinking skills—to have knowledge of the important subjects and not to flame out on academic tests. Around the country, in part due to the COVID-19 lockdowns, many parents have seen both the schools' lack of academic rigor and their anti-American propaganda—and they protest against it. These parents who demand improved academics would no doubt agree with Robert Maynard Hutchins, the Great Books champion, that vocational schools and/or employers providing on-the-job training can readily teach practical skills to young men and women with sharp thinking abilities.

As a clue to answer the question of how parents can take back the control of curriculum design from the interlocking directorate, let's take a look at a powerful historic example given by Andrew Coulson: the contrasting methods of education that prevailed in Athens and Sparta, two famous city-states of ancient Greece.

Education With Parents in Charge

Athens at its best was a democracy in which government regulations played little part. The state required two years of military training, but other than that, it had little role in education. Generally, parents taught young children as much as they were able, after which the children were sent to school. All schools were private. Any educated person was free to set up a school and teach any subjects he wanted to. Because the schools had to compete with each other, two results followed: One was that competition kept the prices affordable for most parents; the other was that to attract customers in a competitive marketplace, schools had to teach subjects the parents demanded. Coulson writes in *Market Education*: "In every respect, from fees charged to subjects taught, the goals of teachers were brought into line with those of students and their families."

There are numerous notable examples of Athenian education. One is the story of the Sophists, a band of roving educators for hire. The Sophists were educational entrepreneurs who sought to monetize their scholarly ability. Coulson points out in his book that because of Athens' privatized educational system, "The Sophists could teach whatever they wanted, however they wanted, so long as there were people interested in their material, and confident in their methods." These traveling educators flourished in many Greek cities, including Athens. But distinctive to Athens were the great schools of philosophy: Plato founded his school, the Academy, which thrived in Athens for centuries. Aristotle, perhaps the greatest philosopher in history, moved there from the boondocks of Macedonia and founded his school, the Lyceum. Because the two great philosophers were wealthy, their schools did not charge a fee. But there were several excellent for-profit schools in the city. One was headed by another noted philosopher, Isocrates, and most likely attracted more students even than did Plato's. And with the government not involved in education, it lacked the power to shut down schools run by teachers who held views that were socially controversial.

One such case was a school run by a woman named Aspasia. As relatively free and advanced as Athens was, women were held to be second-class citizens. Yet, in *Market Education*, Coulson notes: "Defying prejudices of the day, this foreign-born woman set up in Athens teaching philosophy and rhetoric and unabashedly advocated the liberation and education of the city's women." The takeaway? The freedom of the Athenian education system meant that a controversial teacher could stay in business, even if society generally disliked him or her, as long as that teacher could attract enough students. And how did a school attract enough students to make money? By satisfying parents that their child(ren) received a quality education.

Education With the Government in Charge

By contrast, Sparta was a military dictatorship. The state controlled every arena of life, including schooling. Coulson notes in his book: "Every aspect of child-rearing which in Athens was the right and responsibility of parents, was in Sparta the prerogative of the government." Children belonged to the state, which desired none that were sickly or infirm. Babies were brought before government officials and, if deemed unfit, were thrown from a cliff. At age seven, all males were seized and reared in state-controlled dormitories. Parents had no choice in this matter. The children were trained in sports, fighting, and physical endurance. When children were asked a question, an immediate answer was expected; if it came slowly, the child was punished. Academic education was almost nonexistent. Reading was barely taught. Writing and arithmetic were not taught. The children were exposed to the harshest physical conditions they could handle to school their bodies for future warfare. Their minds were left unschooled.

The Results

The educational results in these two societies were predictable. There is no doubt that Athens was an intellectual and cultural center. Of the great philosophers, Socrates and Plato were citizens and Aristotle lived there after relocating from Macedonia. The leading historian, Thucydides, was an Athenian, as were the great writers Sophocles, Euripides, and Aristophanes. But what about the general population? Information about literacy levels in ancient Athens is gained by looking at the reading necessary to participate as a citizen, the writing on pottery of the era, and references to literacy in the works of Athenian writers.

Regarding the overall populace, Coulson writes in *Market Education*: "By all accounts, Athens was the most literate society in the Western world at that time." Overall, Coulson gives us a clear picture regarding Athenian culture: "Athenian parents had complete discretion over the content and manner of their children's education, and those children went on to create a culture responsible for some of the greatest advances in art, science, and human liberty in history."

He points out that the Spartans, on the other hand, "were among the least literate people in ancient Greece, if not the ancient world as a whole." The average citizen had little or no knowledge of reading, writing, or arithmetic. The purpose of Spartan schooling was to train soldiers to serve and fight for the state, not to educate future writers, artists, scientists, businessmen, or informed citizens of a free society. If parents had possessed control over the education of their children, is it likely that the schools would have churned out an army of illiterates trained solely to fight and die for the state? Is this what most parents want for their kids? Perhaps there are some who do. After all, according to legend, Spartan mothers told their warrior sons, "Come home with your shields or on them." Nevertheless, if mothers and not the government had the final say regarding education of their sons—as they should—how many would choose to have their boys ripped from them at age seven and indoctrinated to do nothing but fight and die for the state? Presumably, not many.

Other examples could be given, including from early America (and Coulson's book does give them), but this is enough to show the great educational advantages of parental rather than government control over the schooling of children. Can these lessons be applied today? If so, how? As a first step in answering these questions, let's briefly look at places in the poorest parts of the world today where this policy has positive results.

CHAPTER THIRTEEN

Parents in Charge - Overseas

Malala Yousafzai is the youngest person ever to win the Nobel Peace Prize. She grew up in the Swat Valley of Pakistan, where her father was an educational entrepreneur who founded a low-cost private school. The Taliban, who are prevalent along the Afghani-Pakistani border, are a brutal band of fanatics dead set against women's education. One morning, as Malala was on her way to school, Taliban thugs tried to murder her. Fortunately she survived, went on to gain a degree from Oxford University in England, and became a forthright spokeswoman supporting education for *all children*, girls as well as boys.

The backstory of her accomplishments is extraordinary. Malala's father, Ziauddin, started his private, low-cost school in Mingora, a city in the Swat Valley, in 1994. He had noticed that the government schools were educationally inferior and that there was parental demand for effective private education. He and a friend invested all the money they had (roughly US $1,750) in starting their own center of learning. They had a difficult time of it but succeeded in the long run. James Tooley, the English educational expert, wrote a book on these educational institutions titled, *Really Good Schools*. In it, he reports: "When Malala was born (July 12, 1997), the school fees were PKR [Pakistani currency] 100 per month [or US $2.47]. That's a low-cost private school, accessible to poor families." Ziauddin joined an organization of private schools, became vice president, and fought against political corruption that forced private school owners to pay bribes to government officials. It's quite a success story. Tooley summarizes the achievement in his book: "Against the odds, her father, with four hundred other educational entrepreneurs, has created *private* schools for the poor in a remote region of the world, because even poor parents don't want to accept the mediocrity and abuse of public schools."

Ziauddin Yousafzai created a so-called self-organized school—and thousands of such small schools in the world's poorest nations are the most exciting development in education in decades, perhaps centuries.

Tooley is an outstanding researcher who has revealed to the world an amazing truth. Small, low-cost, private, often for-profit schools are developing *by the thousands and thousands* across the poorest, most war-torn areas of Africa and Asia. These self-organized schools substantially outperform government schools in academic achievement and are widely preferred by parents. Tooley has ventured into the poorest slums and the most remote rural areas of impoverished Third World nations in search of these schools. He has found a seemingly endless supply of them and interviewed both the educational entrepreneurs who run them and the parents of their attending students. The stories he tells are true and inspiring.

For example, Tooley tells the story of how he first discovered a surprising truth on a visit to Hyderabad, India, in 2000. Based on earlier research, he had a hunch of what he might find and ventured into the slums of the Old City. Down an alley, he found a school in a residential building. This was not a school run by the state. It was a low-cost private school that charged US one dollar per month. Then he found another such school, and another, and so forth. He says in *Really Good Schools*, "[Soon] I was connected to the president of a federation of five hundred of these low-cost schools, serving poor and low-income communities across Hyderabad."

Tooley was excited by these findings. Why wasn't this news, given that education is such an important commodity? Why didn't more people in the West know of these many low-cost private schools that poor parents preferred by the thousands to the "free" government schools? He set out to explore this phenomenon and report it to people in the world's wealthier nations.

Tooley tells dozens of these important stories, which should be widely known. Here is another: Kibera, in Nairobi, Kenya, is one of the largest slums in East Africa. Tooley ventured with some children into this impoverished area and found that many of them were in low-cost private schools. "We found more than one hundred low-cost private schools in the slums of Kibera alone," he writes in his book.

In the fishing village of Bortianor, in the region of Ga outside Accra, Ghana, Tooley found seven such private schools as well. A fisherman named Joshua told Tooley that as soon as he and his wife could afford to, they sent their daughter to a private school. Why? Joshua explained: "The reason the private school is better than the public is because there is a private owner. If the teacher doesn't teach as required, he will be fired and replaced." Parents across the world's poorest regions recognize this basic economic truth: Private businesses have competitors. They need to satisfy their customers in order to retain their business; otherwise, they'll lose customers to a rival. Government schools, which gain money by taxation and gain students by compulsory attendance, have no such economic motive to excel. Joshua is absolutely correct.

Tooley gave a talk in China regarding his findings. An Englishman from an international development organization spoke with him after the talk. He said he worked all over China, in both urban and rural areas, and he assured Tooley there were no low-cost private schools in China, that private schooling was exclusively for the rich. He told Tooley: "Perhaps [you] had found low-cost private schools in India or Africa. But in China, there were none."

By this time, Tooley had heard the same story over and again from both government officials and international aid workers. Yet in every country he visited, without exception, he ventured into the slums and poorest rural areas and found numerous low-cost private schools. He journeyed into the poor rural areas of China. With a Chinese graduate student of his, he flew into Lanzhou, the capital of Gansu. They traveled through mountains and over rough trails. They saw peasants working with scythes, harvesting the same way their ancestors had for centuries, perhaps millennia before them. In his book, Tooley reports: "We went through a narrow gorge. There we found our first low-cost private school in the Gansu Mountains: Ming Xin, People's Hearts private school, where the husband-and-wife team greeted us warmly.... Over the next few days, we visited five similar low-cost private schools in these spectacular highlands."

Eventually Tooley organized a large research team, and they explored some of China's mountainous regions. They found 586 low-cost private schools. The international aid workers who claimed there were no such private schools in China's poorest regions were correct...but only to a point. "They [the aid workers] were working in what they considered to be the remotest, poorest villages of Gansu, the poorest province in China. In those villages, it was true, there were no private schools," Tooley says. "But if you pushed farther, traveled for a day beyond those villages, then there were even poorer communities, beyond the reach of the [Communist] state. And there we found the low-cost private schools."

Let's look at one more extreme example. Tooley ventured into Makoko, Nigeria, a slum area constructed on pilings over the brackish waters of Lagos Lagoon. Tooley told his Nigerian host that this was where he wanted to go. His host said "too dangerous," so Tooley went alone. His cab driver also considered the destination too dangerous, so Tooley hired a canoe, paddled in, and found some children. He asked them where they went to school. An eight-year-old girl named Sandra said Ken-ade and took him there. In the end, Ken-ade Private Secondary School was only one of thirty-two private schools Tooley and his team found in Makoko. As mentioned, government officials and employees of developmental aid organizations were almost always skeptical of Tooley's findings. But eventually, he convinced a high-ranking British government official to take a look for himself. On a trip to Nigeria, the official visited Ken-ade. From the school computer, he emailed Tooley: "I am impressed by both the quantity of private schools I have seen, as well as their quality."

Let's talk about the quality of these low-cost private schools, and about several other important factors: 1. the state of the government schools, 2. academic achievement, and 3. overall parental preferences.

The State of the Government Schools

Just as in America, the public school systems in poor nations around the world are doing a terrible job of educating their students. Parents in many poor areas complained bitterly to Tooley about the government schools. For example, the researcher spoke with parents in the town of Kutch, a fishing village in Gujarat, India. One father told him that the children typically arrived at public school around 8:30 in the morning; the teachers generally got there around an hour later and immediately sent the kids home for breakfast. The children got back to school around 10:30 a.m. for assembly, chores, and prayers. After that, the teachers taught for half an hour—or not—and left for the day by noon. The same father said the children learned nothing in the government schools. Another father, a fisherman, said that his son was in the fifth grade and had learned only how to write the number 1—nothing more.

Another father, also a fisherman, went to the school to complain about the lack of education his child was receiving. The teachers called the police and had the fisherman removed from the building. His family had to raise money to pay for his bail and court fees. The school continued as it had before. The father could do nothing about it; he had been taught his place. Speaking of these parents, Tooley writes in *Really Good Schools*: "Like parents I encountered in Liberia, Sierra Leone, and South Sudan, and in India, Nigeria, Kenya, Ghana, and China before that, such parents are not satisfied with the quality of education in public schools. That's an important reason they chose private schools."

Academic Achievement

Do students at the private schools perform better academically? Yes, they certainly do. Tooley cites numerous studies, all of them reporting the same conclusion: The kids attending low-cost private schools in the world's poorest regions consistently do better on academic achievement tests than do kids in government schools. Tooley states: "[C]hildren in the private schools were between 1.5 and 2.5 years ahead of the public school counterparts." Various studies show that the gap between public and private schools regarding academic performance is far greater than for any other factors. For example, the difference in English performance between public school and private school students is twelve times greater than the difference between rich kids and poor ones. In math, the divide between private and public school students is eight times greater than that between kids with literate fathers and those with illiterate ones. Regarding mastery of Urdu (the official national language of Pakistan), the knowledge of private school kids over public school kids is eighteen times greater than that of children with literate mothers over those with illiterate ones.

Tooley writes in his book: "Pupils attending private school tend to achieve better learning outcomes than pupils in state schools." Studies from "South Asia and sub-Saharan Africa...show these results—children in low-cost private schools outperform those in government schools." He summarizes: "A picture is also emerging of some of the major virtues of low-cost private schools. They are serving huge numbers of children, they are affordable, they are of higher quality [than government schools], and are better value for [the] money."

Overall Parental Preferences

It is not surprising that poor parents overwhelmingly prefer to send their children to low-cost private schools. A few studies have asked parents their preference, and the response was nearly universal in favor of private schools. In one research project in Uttar Pradesh, India, 94.4 percent of parents answered in support of private schooling. Tooley points out that "[s]imilar results have been found from many other studies around the world."

Academic achievement is one critical factor with which parents are concerned when choosing a school for their children. There are others. Safety is an issue, including protection from bullying at the hands of both other students and teachers. Proximity to home and transportation to and fro form a constellation of issues. Cost is a major issue, especially for those living in poverty and extreme poverty. But it is striking that parents around the world, including in the poorest regions, are overwhelmingly concerned with academic advancement. Unlike the "educators" who control America's interlocking directorate, parents want their children to read and write effectively, understand math, and master the academic program. They want their children to know facts—information—and to think effectively. This is almost always true.

This is one reason that parents—not governments, and not professional educators—should be in charge of their children's education. They should choose the schools, teachers, and/or tutors who can most effectively educate their children. Parents should and sometimes do recognize that teachers and schools are similar to contractors. Let us say some homeowners want to construct a soundproof office in their basement. They hire a contractor. They tell him what they want. The contractor is the construction expert, and he proceeds to build it for them. But the homeowners set the terms of the project; they specify what is to be built. The contractor works for them.

Similarly, parents should be able to patronize the school that offers what they want their children to learn—or should be able to hire private tutors/teachers to do so. The teachers/tutors are the educational experts and would proceed to educate the kids. But the parents set the terms of the educational project; they specify what is to be taught and the methods to be used. The teachers and the school both work for the parents. In both cases, customers are hiring professionals to do a job—and if the pros do not deliver, the customers can fire them and hire someone who does.

Let's fire the interlocking directorate. Let's circumvent the impregnable fortress. Let's put parents back in charge of American education. How? There are numerous ways.

CHAPTER FOURTEEN

Parents in Charge - at Home

My mother did not graduate from high school. She was intelligent and could read and write, but she was not an enthusiastic reader. Nevertheless, she made "flash cards," small cardboard or index cards on which she handwrote the letters of the alphabet and the sounds they made. She showed the cards to my sisters and me, and we would sound out the letters. In this way, we learned our ABCs. Then she handwrote cards that combined vowels with consonants, and we learned to match the letter combinations with the sounds they made. In other words, she used systematic phonics to teach us the basics of reading. She did the same for the multiplication table, which we memorized. To this day, I can quickly rattle off that nine times five equals forty-five, that eight times nine equals seventy-two, that nine times nine equals eighty-one, and so forth. I am forever grateful to my mother for the head start in education she gave to us at ages four and five.

This story provides a clue to answer the main question of this chapter: What can parents do to take control of their children's education and promote much better results than currently exist? We will come back to my mother's story and the lessons it contains in a bit.

There are a number of things parents can do. The first possibility is homeschooling, which is legal in every state. In the past twenty years or so, homeschooling has become increasingly widespread in the United States. For example, in 2003, some 1,096,000 students were homeschooled. By 2012, as more and more people became fed up with public schools that failed to either serve their children or respond to parental demands, that number had increased to 1,773,000. This represented roughly 3.4 percent of American school students aged five to seventeen.

This percentage held steady until the pandemic of 2020. Many schools moved their classes online, and students worked from home. This gave parents more direct contact with what goes on in their kids' courses, with the dreck that is so often taught and with the disgraceful absence of serious academic content. Presumably, many were troubled by what they saw. The numbers of homeschooled kids began to rise. In the spring of 2020, approximately 5.4 percent of American students were homeschooled; this number rose to 11.1 percent in the fall of 2020. Also by the fall, the percentage of Black American students homeschooled had risen to roughly 16 percent. By June 2021, the number of kids homeschooled in Massachusetts increased by approximately 119 percent over the previous several years. As the pandemic winds down and schools nationwide gradually reopen fully with on-site classes, will these homeschooling gains hold?

We will see. But the impressive academic record achieved by many homeschooled students over the years gives reason to believe that they might. Multiple surveys show that home-schooled students generally outperform public school kids on standardized exams testing knowledge of academic subjects, often by some 30 percentile points. This homeschooler academic superiority is seen on tests including the SATs and other college admission tests. This is not a surprise. The simple truth is that parents generally value academic subjects much more highly than does the interlocking directorate. Consequently, parents teach those subjects more widely and deeply than do many of our public schools.

Many parents realize the educational advantages of homeschooling but have strong doubts about educating their children in this way. They point out, "We are not teachers. We don't have the knowledge or the skills necessary to teach our children." This is certainly an understandable objection. Further, some parents say: "We are so busy at work, making money to feed and support our children, that we simply do not have the time or the energy required to do a good job teaching them." This is also a valid point. How do we address them? One quick response, in all seriousness, is: How good a teacher do you need to be to do a better job than the public schools do? The truth is: not very.

There are different types and amounts of home-schooling. Many parents already homeschool without realizing it. For example, parents who teach their young children the alphabet, the sounds of the letters, the sounds of letter combinations, the rudiments of reading, and the multiplication table—as my mother did—are homeschooling. Similarly, parents who help their kids after school with their math homework, a science project, or a writing assignment are also homeschooling. Educating children at home does not necessarily require pulling the kids out of school. A loving parent might recognize that the schools are not doing their job, and do a great deal of supplemental work at home. Afterschooling, as it is currently called, is a valuable form of homeschooling.

Teaching a Child to Read

The gift of reading is the greatest educational advantage that parents can give their children, for it opens the entire world of knowledge. And it is not that hard to do, even for busy, hardworking parents who are not teachers. Using flash cards is a simple way to teach the kids to sound out letters and, eventually, words. Today it is even easier, because companies like Hooked on Phonics sell products that make it very easy for kids to master the alphabet. Hooked on Phonics offers various apps, games, and workbooks that are both fun and helpful in teaching children to sound out words.

Let me make another point on this issue—and then address what the real problem is for some parents. When my daughter was a child, we would do all kinds of fun things together: go to the park, ride bikes, play catch, play at all kinds of imaginary games that she made up—and we would read. It was very important for her to learn that there are all kinds of cool and fun things in books. If children learn that reading is fun, then they will want to learn to read and not have to depend on Mom or Dad to read to them. So, between trips to the park and other fun places, we went to the bookstore, whether Barnes & Noble or another. We would go to the children's section, and I always let her pick out the book. The important things were that it looked like fun to her and that she was motivated to read it. She is, and has always been, a very careful shopper; at times, she would take a full hour to choose the book she wanted. The books were often goofy stories about a dog that could fly, or a kitten who thought the full moon was a bowl of milk, and so forth. But the key point is that at three or four years old, she found such stories fun. She would sit on the floor of the children's section, pat the floor next to her, and say: "Sit down, Daddy, and read to me." And I did.

There are two very important things that all parents can do to make sure their children learn the key task of all education—learning to read well: 1. Show the kids at a very young age that reading is fun. 2. Use systematic phonics to teach them how to do it. This is a type of homeschooling. All parents can do this for their children—and it is not that hard.

The hard part may be dealing with the schools. Because the interlocking directorate is often against the use of phonics, the schools very often do not use it. There are times when the teachers will not allow students to sound out words; times when they forbid it even with *children who already know how to read*; times when they insist the children use some version of the whole-word method. This is a real problem that some parents have to face. Their child wants to and should be able to trust the teacher, but in these cases, the teacher is dead wrong and is teaching a poor method that creates millions of semi-illiterates. How should responsible parents handle this problem? The best thing is to pull a child from such a school and educate him or her at home. But for parents who cannot do that, what is the next best thing?

The child will certainly be confused if Mom and Dad tell him or her one thing and the teacher demands the opposite. In such a case, this confusion is sadly unavoidable. Reading is too important a skill for the parents to allow the schools to mess it up for their son or daughter. If necessary, the parents must confront the teacher, the principal, or the PTA, and insist that their child be allowed to sound out new words when reading. If the school will not allow it, then at the very least, the parents must tell the child: "You know how to read. Don't let the teacher confuse you. Sounding out new words is the right method." The parents need to stand tall for their child's education.

It is true that the teacher-student relationship is important—but the parent-child relationship is much more important. If parents have established a loving relationship with their child in his or her first five or six years before going to school, the child will trust Mom and Dad's judgment—especially when he or she can already read and sees that sounding words out is the method that works. This truth is driven home even more forcefully when the child notices that the whole-word method teaches other children to read only very slowly and painfully…if at all.

Hiring Tutors

There is another possible aspect of homeschooling: tutors. Parents might think that hiring tutors is expensive, but this is not necessarily the case, especially given the technology available today. Consider that there are graduate students across the country who are studying for a PhD in every academic field. They hold a bachelor's degree in their field—in college, they majored in their field, not in education—which means they already know more about the subject than do most high school teachers. Plus, they might already have completed two to three years of graduate study, again in their field, which places them well beyond most high school teachers. And because they are full-time students, they do not yet hold a full-time job. This means that most of them have little money. Many are searching for ways to make money by using their knowledge in their field. Tutoring kids in their area of expertise is a perfect way for them to do so. And because they are just starting in their career, they are not yet known and their prices are relatively low. The grad students also realize that in addition to the money they make tutoring, they are gaining valuable teaching experience, are adding to their résumé, and, if they do a good job, can get a strong reference from the parents.

There is much value for a grad student in tutoring. And, in a certain way, it is even better for them than teaching a course or two part-time at a local college (which I did when I was a graduate student). Very often, those teaching college courses need to travel to the school. This involves time, gas money or carfare, and wear and tear on both you and your car; and it is tiring. (I drove or took trains and buses all over the New York City area, traveling like an academic gypsy from college to college. I handwrote with a pen and notebook large parts of my doctoral dissertation while sitting in my car in a college parking lot before class. It was not fun—but it was necessary. You pay your dues, right?) But with the technology available today, grad students can tutor kids working from their computers at home *and can find students anywhere in the country and even in other parts of the world.*

Parents can use a number of online tools to find a tutor who is right for their kids. They can search on LinkedIn. They can advertise on Facebook and Twitter. They can go to websites of homeschooling parents to see if they recommend tutors. They can contact homeschooling organizations. They can do a Google search for tutors either local or remote. One promising company is Varsity Tutors, which offers many tutors and teachers in a wide array of subjects. It provides one-on-one tutoring and has small and larger classes as well.

Referrals and networking are good possibilities. For example, let's say a parent finds a tutor by one of the above means, but the tutor's schedule is booked. The parent can ask the tutor if he or she knows of any others who have great knowledge in the field. This is how I got my first teaching job at C.W. Post Campus of Long Island University in Greenvale, New York. The chair of the philosophy department at Post asked a Post graduate (who was a friend of mine) if he wanted to teach a course at his alma mater. His schedule was filled; the chair asked if he knew anybody who would be good; my friend recommended me; the chair called me and offered me the job. I accepted, and my teaching career was born. The same type of networking and referrals works for finding tutors. So there are many ways by which parents can find and hire experts.

As an example, a friend of mine in Minnesota named Melanie Hoffman homeschooled her three children. As part of their advanced education, she hired tutors for them. I am one of the tutors she hired; I taught her kids both literature and philosophy. I asked if she would answer questions regarding tutoring, and she generously agreed. Here is my question-and-answer session with her.

1. **Why did you decide to homeschool your children?**

   The main reason was the state of education in the public (government) schools. They were—and still are—a huge disappointment to me. They imbue children with complex political ideas such as environmentalism, socialism, anticapitalism, and anti-America rhetoric before they even have the ability to process them properly—as found in today's schools teaching critical race theory. The appalling lack of independent thinking being taught in the government schools really made my decision an easy one. To state it more positively, I wanted to encourage my children to think for themselves. I wanted them to embrace learning and to know the power of their own mind, using it fully to understand and embrace the world around them and to be able to understand objective reality. I had only one chance to give my children the best education I could, to fully maximize their learning potential, and public education was not going to accomplish that.

2. What caused you to decide to hire tutors?

I reached a point where I had exhausted my "expertise" and really needed to enlist some individuals who specialized in their field. A loving parent generally can give his or her children the basics of a good education. A parent can use systematic phonics to teach reading, can show the kids how to write grammatical sentences, then paragraphs, and eventually a complete essay. The parents can teach arithmetic. They can teach history—the basics of American history and of world history. There are good simple history texts they can read to gain the information to pass on to the young children. But at a certain point, you know you will arrive at an educational place beyond your knowledge. Before you arrive at that place, you prepare by starting a search for expert tutors.

3. Did you teach the children yourself when they were younger and then decide on tutors—or did you hire tutors immediately?

In most subjects I taught them until junior high, then hired tutors. I knew my limitations. I wanted my children to soar in their education and in their lives, so I hired experts to take them to the next level.

4. How did you find suitable tutors? Do they advertise? Did you find them online? Did you advertise? If so, where?

Being part of a philosophy group with other like-minded individuals, I asked them for referrals and found some wonderful teachers—many of whom still teach my children today. But there are tutoring sites to which parents can go for this kind of information. One is the website of Varsity Tutors.

5. In which subjects did you hire tutors?

Math, philosophy, history, literature, and science. Obviously, I wanted to give my kids an outstanding academic education, and so I hired tutors who are experts in these fields.

6. How did the tutoring work out? Are you satisfied with the results?

The tutoring, all online from the beginning, worked out better than I imagined. The teachers knew that teaching online required developing and holding the children's interest in the material by interacting with them, making participation an enjoyable part of the class. It never felt like the teachers were hundreds of miles away. I was able to sit in on a lot of classes—in the background, of course—and I saw firsthand how qualified the tutors are. My kids learned a great deal from them—and so did I.

7. What was the main benefit of hiring tutors?

One thing I liked was that it was still home-school learning, since we were all home together. A number of homeschool parents choose to do this because the public schools often have problems with bullies, crim-inals, and drugs. There are no such prob-lems at home. But I also really appreciated the fact that I could employ experts in their field from anywhere in the country! Our history and science teachers live in Texas, our philosophy teacher is in New York, our literature teacher is from North Carolina, and our math class was online this year from a local university! It would've been quite a commute if it weren't for the amazing online technology at our fingertips.

8. **With the public schools a terrible mess, would you recommend to parents the use of tutors to educate their children?**

Absolutely, without hesitation. I think all parents want to give their children a good education, but as far back as they can remember everyone has sent their children to school somewhere, to be taught by someone, using methods unfamiliar to the parents. It's been taken for granted that public schools are the source of education. I recommend getting involved in your child's education, at whatever level you are comfortable. Whether it be hiring one tutor or many, or homeschooling them yourself, the insight into your child's education is invaluable, as is the education your child will receive. It is a great advantage to have your children tutored by someone who is expert in his or her subject rather than by a teacher whose degree is in education, not in the subject he or she teaches.

9. **That was my next question: Do tutors generally know their subject better than public school teachers do?**

From my experience, the answer is yes. Granted, I didn't enroll my children in public school, but as a private music teacher, through my interactions with children who attended public school, I was shocked at how little some of them knew and how low their reading levels were. I see many examples of how poorly educated a large number of public school students are—and it makes me sad.

10. Is it very expensive to hire tutors?

It can add up, but it doesn't come close to the cost of a private school education, nor the cost of missing the chance to give your child the education they deserve. Great tutors can be found, and I think they're worth every penny. I once saw a car bumper sticker that read: "If you think education is expensive, try ignorance." A good education for your children is priceless. I would look for a second job if that was needed to pay for the kids' tutors.

11. Are there online or social media sites where parents can go to find suitable tutors?

The children's history teacher hosted some of his classes through Outschool. This is an education platform designed for home learning. We started taking other courses on Outschool, including classes in art, government, grammar, coding, and science. Their website states that they offer one hundred thousand interactive online classes—and that they teach students from age three to age eighteen. We were pleased with the results. I recommend contacting them.

12. **Are you willing to share any contact information where parents can reach you with questions about homeschooling and/or hiring tutors?**

I'd be happy to help! I encourage anyone with questions to contact me. Parents can reach me at aynrandstudygroup@gmail.com.

13. **As a successful homeschooling parent, do you have any final thoughts for parents regarding the education of their children?**

Mainly this: You can do it! You can make a difference! In speaking with other parents, I have found the number-one reason parents shy away from getting more involved in their children's education is lack of confidence. "Oh, I could never do that!" is a comment

I have heard many times. It may not be for everyone, that is true, but I would encourage parents to weigh the benefits of taking a more active role in their children's education. It may be just hiring a tutor, or several, to enhance and supplement the public education they are receiving, or it might be fully embracing the challenge themselves to educate their children. But whatever level of involvement a parent is comfortable with, it will be an invaluable step in giving your child a chance at reaching their full potential.

14. Have your homeschoolers taken standardized tests? If so, how did they do?

Yes, all three of my children have taken standardized tests since they were in grade school. As homeschoolers, we are required by the state of Minnesota to do so. They have always done very well. As an example, take the SATs. My oldest son, now a freshman in college, scored a 1570 out of 1600 on his SAT last year. My sixteen-year-old daughter also took the SAT and scored 1510. My youngest son, thirteen years old, took the PSAT and scored 1240 out of a possible 1440. My oldest son was accepted at two-thirds of the colleges to which he applied. I have always thought that standardized tests were a good

way to measure my children's progress—
indicating where their strengths lie in some
areas and where there is room for improve-
ment in others.

Who Watches the Kids?

There is another question regarding tutors that must be
addressed. Melanie Hoffman, as a private music instructor,
can often set her own hours; so she can be at home super-
vising her children, which was especially important when
they were young. But what about parents who work away
from home? If the kids are at home studying with tutors
online, who looks after them? Babysitters are necessary—but can often be expensive and, worse, unreliable.
The good news is that the best babysitters are often free.
For example, in a number of cases, parents have family
members, close friends, and/or neighbors that live close
by. The mother and father of one or both of the parents
are possible babysitters; a brother or sister who works
from home is sometimes possible; a close friend or trusted
neighbor that homeschools or works remotely might be
able to look after the tutored kids while they study on their
laptops. Today, more people are able to work from home.
Perhaps one of the parents might be able to do so. There
are a variety of viable options. Let me quote my maternal
grandfather, who, as an immigrant to this country, held
both a strong work ethic and a positive can-do spirit.
"There's always a way to do something," he used to say.
With enough determination, yes, there is.

Traditional Homeschooling

Then there is the traditional homeschooling option, by which one of the parents educates the children, at least in the early grades. Let's refer to an excellent little book by Laura Kronen, a homeschooling mother previously mentioned. Its title is *Homeschool Happily*. Kronen tells the true story of how she came to homeschool her two sons, the difficulties the family faced, and the triumphs they all achieved. She shows other parents that it can be done—and that it is worth doing. First, she points out the many reasons that parents pull their children from the public schools and teach them at home. The reasons are worth repeating. One is the various dangers that lurk in the schools—bullying is common, crime is a legitimate concern in urban areas, and the possibility of school invasion is real. Drugs are also widespread in many schools, including in almost all affluent suburban areas. Another key reason is superior academics at home.

In *Homeschool Happily*, Kronen also tells prospective homeschooling parents the reason for this academic superiority: "There is no school better than a loving and encouraging home." Obviously, in an overwhelming number of cases, Mom and Dad love their kids more than do teachers, administrators, and bureaucrats of the interlocking directorate. *They care more about the child's education.* They also know the specific interests of the child better—if young Tommy or Sarah prefers reading or math; if he or she will pursue engineering, medicine, literature, or another field; if he or she has robust energy that must find an outlet between bouts of study, and so forth. Further, the parent does not have a classroom of twenty students or more; he or she has a small number of children and can devote a generous portion of one-on-one instruction to them.

In 2021, the National Home Education Research Institute (NHERI) published an essay by Brian Ray titled, "Research Facts on Home Schooling," which is available at the National Home Education Research Institute. In the essay, Ray claimed that homeschooled students typically scored "15 to 30 percentile points above public school students on standardized academic achievement tests." The above points are among the reasons why. Further, it is very likely that most homeschooling parents employ systematic phonics to teach reading, which is the single most important academic skill for any person. This gives homeschooled children an enormous educational advantage, for it opens to them the entire world of knowledge. Remember: The elementary years are the most important years of a person's education, for it is then that the foundations are laid. If children are taught the whole-word method, rather than systematic phonics, their ability to read will be undermined, with harmful consequences for any future education.

There are many resources available for homeschooling parents, including curricula and methods to prioritize the order in which material is taught. Indeed, we will devote an entire chapter to these. But first, we should discuss homeschool co-ops.

Homeschool Co-ops

Homeschool co-ops generally are formed by a group of homeschooling parents who pool their resources. They operate a school in one of the parents' homes or in a space they rent—for example, churches, which are often empty on weekdays and usually inexpensive to lease. The parents teach the students in the field(s) they know best; on some occasions, they might hire a teacher. The website TheHomeSchoolMom helpfully covers these co-ops.

On the website Parents, Nicole Johnson states:

> *Another option for a co-op includes several parents working within the confines of a set curriculum to educate their children together. They often switch off, whether by subject or day, and take turns educating each other's children. This "it takes a village" approach helps parents by shifting and sharing the responsibility of educating their kids. The one caveat is that in certain [geographic] areas, parents are not allowed to homeschool other people's children. For example, in Washington D.C., no one other than a parent or guardian may provide homeschool instruction to their children. It is important for parents interested in this type of co-op to check into their state's education department homeschool laws and requirements. This can be done with a simple internet search.*
>
> *There is another homeschool co-op option for parents looking to leave their children's education to certified teachers. Often, several families join together and hire a teacher.*

This allows for a sharing of costs as well as camaraderie and socialization. [What one mother] foresees for her own family is very specific. She hopes for three to four families with children similar in ages/grades to get together for a couple of hours each day in the morning, five days a week. "I envision a condensed learning time for a portion of the day and then the remainder of the day be free play/chores, assigned homework, reading, etc.,"' she says.

Such a co-op is a great option for parents who already have decided to homeschool.

Private Schools Founded by a Certified Teacher

My buddy Mike Gustafson shows another way to circumvent the impregnable fortress. He was certified to teach elementary school in Massachusetts and did so for several years, using phonics to teach reading. Not surprisingly, his students were the best readers in the school. Mike and his wife, Iara, are admirers of Maria Montessori and used her methods to teach their own children. Several years in a public elementary school were enough for Mike; he and Iara opened their own school, Atlas Academy. Here is a description from the school's website:

Atlas Academy began three years ago as a school that Mike and Iara Gustafson started to build for their two children. Now, in its

> *third year, there are over sixty students in four classrooms. Atlas Academy is a Montessori school, which means that we follow the Montessori approach, hire Montessori teachers, and use Montessori curriculum materials. The Montessori approach is an individualized approach to education which helps children to learn and grow at their own pace and cultivates a love of learning.*

We know that Montessori's methods are highly effective for teaching young children. But I bring this up for another reason. *Because he is a certified teacher, the state of Massachusetts only minimally obstructed his goal of starting a private school.* Related, in the past year or so, I have read social media accounts of other public school teachers opting out of the system, contracting with a few disgruntled families, and setting up a small private school to teach the children of those families. This small community-school approach is another option to improve education. All it takes is a few parents to hire a certified teacher and set up a small school in somebody's basement, rec room, or an inexpensive rented space. Remember that this is very similar to how the great Marva Collins got started. A private teacher might not be a magnificent educator à la Marva Collins, but in order to improve on the public schools, he or she does not have to be. Some states make it more difficult than others to start a private school, but certified teachers can always do it. One advantage of many that small community schools enjoy, similar to homeschools, is the relatively small number of students in each class, permitting a great deal of individualized instruction.

In November 2021, the business magazine *Forbes* published an important essay titled "Got Teacher Burnout? Launch a Microschool," by Kerry McDonald, available at Forbes.com. The main point of the article is that a number of effective teachers are fed up with the stifling bureaucracy of the public schools but, passionate about teaching, want to remain in the profession; so they are starting their own small community schools. Because many parents are similarly disgusted with the public schools, these dedicated teachers find families that prefer the microschool approach for their children. McDonald's essay recommends A.SCHOOL, "a learning management platform for teachers who are creating microschools." McDonald also discusses Prenda, an Arizona-based company that currently "enrolls nearly 3,000 learners [at many sites] across Arizona, Colorado, Kansas, Louisiana, and New Hampshire." The takeaway from the essay is that such educational marriages between disgusted teachers and dissatisfied parents are increasingly taking place across the nation—and properly so. (And to be clear about the terminology: The word "microschool" is just a fancy current term for a small community school of the type we've been discussing.)

A good question can be raised at this point: If certified teachers are generally as bad as I've been saying throughout, why should parents send their children to a microschool started by one? There are two parts to the answer: 1. Teachers who form a microschool are probably a self-selecting group—that is, those most dedicated to teaching and most frustrated by the public schools' anti-academic bias. 2. *Parents of children at a private microschool are paying customers*. If they deem the teacher's knowledge insufficient, they can demand the teacher upgrade it... or lose their business. Remember: Elementary education is the most fundamental level of schooling; and it is not that difficult for a teacher to gain the knowledge of the basics—the traditional three Rs of reading, writing, and arithmetic—that's necessary to effectively teach young children. Another point is that some of us are friendly with people who know a great deal of various important subjects. As an illustration, here are some people I know well: 1. a retired elementary school teacher with decades of experience teaching younger grades, 2. a scientist who, when he retired, briefly taught science in school before leaving because of the chaos in the public schools, 3. an aviation engineer who briefly taught math before leaving the public schools for the same reason, 4. a former teacher with a math degree from the Massachusetts Institute of Technology (MIT) who tutors students in his field, and 5. someone with a PhD in American history who has taught science to bright sixth graders.

I myself have taught high school English courses, and volunteered to work in literature with twelve-year-old students at my daughter's Montessori school. I am sure I could think of other such persons who have a great deal of knowledge. Some of these knowledgeable people may be happy to share their expertise with children of different ages. Some of them may be certified teachers. If they are certified teachers, starting a small private school will be much easier for them, as mentioned; whether they are or they aren't, they may be good candidates to tutor either in person or online.

Also, if some intelligent, caring person wants to teach history, let us say, to elementary school students, but does not yet know a lot of history, it is not that difficult to go on the website of either Amazon or Barnes & Noble and find several solid books for beginners on the subject. For example, I just searched on Amazon for "American history made simple," and a bunch of books came up. The budding history teacher can buy one or two, study them over the summer, and be prepared to teach it to the children—and provide them with much more knowledge than they would get in the public schools. The same is true of basic science. The Usborne Beginners Series Science Collection is one collection of books from which to possibly learn enough basic science to teach young children.

More About Microschools

Forming a small community school in some parent's home also removes the problem of violence that troubles the public schools.

Arianna Prothero wrote an essay titled "What Is a Microschool? And Where Can You Find One?" It is available at the Education Week website, identified in the bibliography. In it, she writes:

Microschools—private schools with sometimes as few as a half-dozen students—are popping up in places from Silicon Valley to Washington, D.C.

And along the way, they've been generating excitement inside school-choice circles and tech and business publications like Wired and Fast Company.

Some experts predict microschools have the potential to not only revive the one-room schoolhouse idea of yore but also shake up the private school sector by offering parents a highly personalized education for their children at lower cost than traditional private schools.

A school with only half a dozen students can be very appealing to children and their parents. Each child gets a great deal of individual attention, the discipline problems that trouble many public schools can be easily avoided or ended, and the cost of operating such a school is relatively low, so the price charged per family can be reduced.

One resource for interested parents and teachers is Microschool Revolution. Here is a quote from the company's website:

Microschools are the result of rethinking the traditional educational model to better prepare children for the future. They are small, private institutions where students are empowered to personalize their own educations and are held accountable for their own progress. Often described as "outsourced homeschooling," they are free from the bureaucracy, standardized tests, and mandatory curriculum that defines today's public school system. Microschools tend to be efficiently run, and student engagement is remarkably high.

Any intelligent, motivated person can establish a microschool. Motives for entering the world of personalized education vary. Some people want to escape the inefficiencies of the public system. Others want to give better opportunities to their children. Many want to make a meaningful career nurturing young minds. All of these are excellent reasons, and Microschool Revolution is here to help you along the way.

Individuals who have started their own microschools often provide advice to others on how to do it. Manisha Snoyer is one example. She tells the story of forming a microschool to teach French and acting. After a great deal of hard work, her school was successful; she then founded a company to help others do the same. She wrote a brief essay titled "How I started my own microschool and you can too," available at her blog under the same title.

In the essay, she writes: "This is the story of my journey from artist—to teacher—to entrepreneur—to founding a company that helped teachers start microschools and developing more options for families hoping to personalize their child's education." In the essay, she also provides contact information for those who want to start a microschool of their own.

Here is another success story. In the 1990s, Lisa VanDamme founded her own school in Alisa Viejo, California. She started with one family and two students. Today, VanDamme Academy is a flourishing school with some 130 students and a full K–8 program. On the school's website, she tells of her reasons for starting a school.

Our Story by Lisa VanDamme

VanDamme Academy began twenty-five years ago, with a message on my answering machine.

The message was from a family in Southern California, who were looking for a private, homeschool teacher for their two children and who had heard from a mutual friend that I might be a good candidate for the job.

At the time, I was pursuing an MA in Education at Penn State, with the plan of teaching literature to high school students. Running my own little one-room schoolhouse was not something I had ever contemplated as a career path—it was not something I had even dreamed of. It took one sleepless night to decide that that was exactly what I wanted to do.

Lisa VanDamme started with two students and built her school into a much larger and flourishing institution. But for various reasons, some teachers and families prefer to keep their school tiny—no more than ten students. They do not advertise, they stay off the public radar, and at times, to maintain their small and cozy status, they turn away families. Here is an example of a microschool started by a woman of my acquaintance who was determined to provide a superior education for her children. We'll call her Sarah (not her real name). She was in her late twenties and had a degree in English—not in education—from a local college. She had two young children, a boy and a girl, and as a conscientious mother stayed home to provide them full-time care as her husband worked a steady job. She looked into the local public schools, which she herself had attended as a girl, and was extremely dissatisfied. She convinced her husband that their children would not receive a quality education there and that they should look elsewhere. Sarah spoke with a number of her friends, neighbors, and relatives and found that many of them were not happy with the education their children were receiving in the public schools or dreaded sending their kids there. In addition, a number of parents expressed concern regarding the bullying and drug use there. Some of those unhappy parents considered homeschooling, but with both parents holding full-time jobs deemed it not practical. The idea of forming a small community school came up, and Sarah volunteered to be the teacher. They lived in a state that placed relatively few legal roadblocks in the path of nonteachers starting a small school. They agreed on a sum of money that Sarah would be paid, one family volunteered their basement, they purchased whiteboards and other equipment, and Sarah prepared for her new career. She had received strong training in the humanities and was very able to teach the grade-school kids reading, writing, literature, and history.

But she had never been a great math student. So she spent months boning up on basic arithmetic—long division, decimals, and percentages, and so forth—and on the basics of science as well. She knew there were many books for beginners in a field—the For Dummies series, for instance—and started with those. First, she went through Danica McKellar's *Kiss My Math: Showing Pre-Algebra Who's Boss* and then she read Allan Bluman's *Pre-Algebra Demystified*. She did all the exercises provided in these books. By the time she was done, she had the knowledge to teach basic arithmetic to early elementary school students. Sarah did most of the teaching; a few years later, the parents hired a second teacher with a bachelor's degree in chemistry (not in education) to teach science and advanced math courses. The kids were at ease in a comfortable setting in a furnished basement, with a small number of students, and with a conscientious, strict but caring teacher. The great majority of Sarah's students did very well. This is a common result in small private schools.

I did a quick Google search for "Are there many small private schools?" I found that there are 34,576 private schools in the United States, serving some 5.7 million prekindergarten through twelfth-grade students. Most of them are small. Indeed, 87 percent have enrollments of fewer than 300 students. In the fall of 2015, private schools had an average 166 students enrolled, in contrast to public schools, where the average enrollment was 526 students...more than triple the amount in the average private school. Because some famous private schools have much larger enrollments, this means that there are many that teach far fewer students. Small community schools are definitely an option for parents who are fed up with the public schools but who do not have the time to home-school their children.

Think about it: Self-organized schools in the poorest nations around the globe are doing a better job educating children than are America's public schools. We have seen the reasons why. With all of the advantages that we have—greater wealth, technology, housing, available transportation—can we not duplicate the outstanding academic results achieved in the self-organized schools of numerous Asian and African nations? Of course we can. It is simply a matter of millions of parents deciding we have had enough of the mediocre performance of the public schools, of the inter-locking directorate's stranglehold on American schooling, of the impregnable fortress' refusal to change its educational policies, and perhaps above all, of the so-called professional educators telling us—the children's parents—to butt out, to mind our own business, and to leave the education of our children to the "experts." It is a matter of parents firing the interlocking directorate, circumventing the impregnable fortress, and taking rightful control over the education of our children.

There is also something related that can be done to greatly improve American schooling both in general, and specifically, to encourage a huge growth in the formation of small community schools.

That something would be the bold stroke of abolishing the public schools and fully privatizing the American educational system.

CHAPTER FIFTEEN
The Educational Bonanza of Privatizing Government Schools

Remember these facts about American educational history previously mentioned? In Philadelphia between 1740 and 1776, 125 private schoolmasters advertised their teaching services in the city's newspapers—in a city whose population was tiny back then compared to our day. Thomas Paine's book *Common Sense*, presenting complex political ideas, sold 120,000 copies to a free population of roughly 2.4 million; this is akin to selling ten million copies today. The essays of *The Federalist*, highly advanced arguments written by Hamilton, Madison, and Jay in support of ratifying the US Constitution, *were largely newspaper editorials, read by Everyman and Everywoman*. In the early nineteenth century, the novels of James Fenimore Cooper and Sir Walter Scott—not easy reading—sold millions of copies to a US population of roughly twenty million. McGuffey's Readers were the books used to teach millions of American elementary school children; their material was vastly more advanced than what is used in those grades today.

The evidence is clear: Prior to the mid-nineteenth century establishment of public schools, American education was outstanding and literacy levels were high. It can be so again.

It is time to put on the table for discussion the radical step of abolishing public schools in America and making all education private. There are many points to be made on behalf of such an approach. Let's start with the difficulties of the public schools. The many problems of public schools include the way they are funded, their lack of competition and economic incentive, the fact that children are forced to attend them, the schools' unaccountability regardless of performance, and various other conflicts inherent in a school system based on force.

Local, state, and federal governments finance the public schools by seizing wealth from productive persons, largely via property taxes, but also by means of sales and income taxes, both personal and corporate. So the schools are funded not voluntarily, based on merit, but by coercion, regardless of merit. The public schools do not need to educate well to receive money; they continue to receive taxpayers' dollars regardless of how poorly they educate their students.

Indeed, on the idea that poor academic performance can be fixed primarily by increased spending, the public schools receive *ever more money*, not less, as their educational product worsens. New York City in 2003, for example, made an attempt to improve its public schools by spending an additional seven billion dollars on them. Everyone involved was horrified by the 2007 NAEP tests, which showed only a small amount of improvement in some areas and continued decline in others.

The gradual collapse of the public schools means ever higher taxes for the honest working persons forced to support them. The government says, in effect: "We are not robbing honest persons enough. We must rob them even more heavily to get funds for our failing schools."

For many families, the taxes they pay to support the government schools make it impossible for them to send their children to a private school, for they are financially unable to pay twice for education. Making matters worse, truancy laws mandate that children attend school until age sixteen. This combination of coercive policies means that many students are *forced* to attend public schools.

The current arrangement makes the public school system akin to a monopoly, in that it is impervious to competition.

By analogy, suppose the government were to establish and run an automobile company; legally require all adults to own a car, which they would receive "free" of charge; and, by means of property, sales, and income taxes, finance the car producer, thus making it monetarily impossible for millions of Americans to purchase a privately manufactured automobile. Such a "business" would gain its income and "customers" by means of a rights-violating system—by both robbing taxpayers and forcing "customers" to own a car—and it would receive the same income and customers regardless of whether its customers deemed its product satisfactory. The car producer would lack any and all economic incentive to excel; no matter how woeful its product, it would be kept in business by wealth taken by force from taxpayers. This is what the government school system does in the much more important field of education.

The Irresolvable Problems of Government Schools

Further, government schools create irresolvable conflicts regarding curricula, textbooks, and teacher training. In order for the government to ensure that its schools are providing government-quality education, the state would need to establish an agency—call it the Bureau of Schooling to oversee the schools, curricula, textbooks, and teacher training. Who would control the bureau? In a dictatorship, the government would control it, and would employ the state schools to ram propaganda down the throats of its subjects. In a mixed economy, such as modern America's, competing interest groups would vie to gain control of the bureau, seeking to impose their preferred educational standards on the nation's youth.

Consider just a few of the conflicts arising from the current American system. Some groups want schools to teach critical race theory—that America is racist through and through, and that white people are inherently racist—while others strenuously object to ramming such propaganda down the throats of children. Some groups want schools to teach evolution; others want them to teach creationism; still others want them to teach both. Some want schools to teach the "virtues" of socialism and the "crimes" of capitalism; others want them to teach the virtues of freedom and the unprecedented accomplishments of America. Some groups want the schools to adopt systematic phonics as the method of teaching reading; others want them to use look-say or some other variant of the whole-word method.

Such conflicts follow necessarily from the coercive method by which government schools are funded, populated, and operated.

Private Schools Not Afflicted by These Problems

By contrast, none of these problems beset private schools. It is common knowledge that private schools are generally academically superior to government schools, and this superiority is borne out on various tests. For instance, in the area of reading, private school fourth graders scored nineteen points higher than their government school counterparts on the 1994 NAEP exam. Likewise, in the field of math, also during the 1990s, the disparity between private school and government school average achievement was equivalent to 3.2 years of learning over the course of high school. A decade later, in 2008, educational researcher Andrew Coulson reported on a comprehensive study—analyzing twenty-five years of educational research from eighteen nations—that compared government schools to private schools. Coulson writes in *Market Education*: The analysis demonstrated not merely the academic superiority of private education but, more revealingly, that "the private sector's margin of superiority is greatest when looking at the least regulated, most market-like private schools." ("Least regulated" means, of course, least dominated by the government, while "most market-like" means having to respond to the demands of customers—that is, the parents.) Coming closer to our own day, a March 2019 essay titled, "New Study Confirms That Private Schools Are No Better than Public Schools," was published at the Public School Review website. Despite the misleading title, the essay states: "Studies show as well that private school students consistently score higher on standardized tests and college entrance exams." As already seen, the findings of James Tooley demonstrate the superiority of private schooling to government schooling on a worldwide scale.

One school that demonstrated both the superiority of the private model and the problems for private schools posed by the government monolith was Westside Preparatory School in Chicago, founded by Marva Collins in 1975. Recall that Collins was a schoolteacher in Chicago who, frustrated by the bureaucratic restrictions of the government schools, resigned and opened Westside Prep. She took in many low-income and minority children deemed incorrigibly uneducable by the same government schools she had fled—and she transformed them into consummate students. She jettisoned the whole-word method of teaching reading used in the government schools, taught systematic phonics instead, and made reading a vital part of every aspect of her curriculum, including mathematics. She did not organize classes based exclusively on age, but let students progress as rapidly as they were able and used advanced students to assist in the teaching of novices. Both she and her school became justly famous for the academic excellence achieved by their students.

Unfortunately, due to insufficient enrollment and funding, Westside Prep closed in 2008—while government schools in Chicago continued to receive both students and funding by means of government use of force. Countless comparisons of private schools to government schools reveal that the former generally outperform the latter. The question is, why?

The main reason is that private schools are *immune* to the problems that inescapably plague government schools. A private school cannot force customers to purchase its product, nor can it compel anyone to finance its existence, nor can it regulate or curtail the activities of its competitors. Because private schools are legally forbidden to use force, their existence and programs entail no violation of rights. Having to earn their customers and money, private schools possess a strong economic incentive to provide excellent educational services. If they want to stay in business and flourish, they must make money by satisfying the educational requirements of students and their families; if they fail to do so, they face bankruptcy. (Even nonprofit private schools must compete for students and funding. If they fail to deliver a satisfactory educational product, families send their children to a competitor that does. And if they fail to succeed in their stated mission, their philanthropic financiers will find other venues for their philanthropy.)

Further, private schools pose no irresolvable problems of curriculum, textbooks, or teaching methods. The *owners* of private schools decide what subjects will be taught, the methods by which they will be taught, and the price at which they will offer their services. Parents voluntarily purchase the services for their children (or not) and continue to purchase them only if satisfied with them and their price. If a private school chooses to teach critical race theory to its students, it is free to do so, and parents are free to decide if they want that for their children. If a private school chooses to reject critical race theory, it is free to do so, and parents can decide if that want *that* for their children. If a private school chooses to focus on the three Rs to the exclusion of painting, music, or drama, it is free to do so, and potential customers are free to patronize the school or not. If another private school chooses to focus on the arts, or to focus on trade skills, or to offer any variety of subjects, it is free to do so, and potential customers are free to do business there or not.

The philosophy of education is complex and controversial, and people's needs and values can differ in countless ways. In a system of private schools, all parents are free to decide what they will do with their money and where they will educate their children; no one is forced to finance schools deemed unworthy or to patronize ideas deemed false or immoral. In short, private schools do not violate rights by initiating force against innocent persons; thus they are free of the myriad problems that accompany rights violations. In other words, private schools are not only moral but also—and consequently—*practical*.

Private schools in America have provided and continue to provide high-quality education. Unfortunately, however, they constitute less than 11 percent of America's educational system today. According to the National Center for Educational Statistics, in the school year 2009–2010, nearly 49.8 million students attended government schools, while 5.8 million were enrolled in private schools. By 2019, roughly 5 million American students were attending private schools, in comparison to some 50 million attending government schools. Because of the numerous coercive laws earlier discussed, approximately 90 percent of American children are *compelled* to attend educationally crippling government schools. This is not merely a tragedy. It is a manmade tragedy; indeed, an atrocity. What is the solution?

The Main Political Solution

One key political solution to the abysmal state of education in America is, as mentioned, to privatize the government schools. For an indication of what would happen to education in America if that were to occur, consider the industries that are either fully or essentially private. Examine the quality, availability, and prices of automobiles, cell phones, CDs, MP3 players, jeans, breakfast cereals, and pain relievers. Consider the quality, availability, and prices of services such as hairstyling, car repair, plumbing, and dentistry. If we focus on any one of these, we can see that the private nature of the businesses involved is what drives quality up and prices down and makes such a diverse array of goods and services available to millions.

For instance, when was the last time anyone complained about a shortage of high-quality, low-priced computers? Countless varieties of personal computers, optional features, and add-ons are available to purchase. It is similar with smart phones. Just over a century and a quarter ago, people had no telephone service. Now they have phones—and high-powered computers—in their pockets! Why are computers so inexpensive, technologically advanced, and abundant? The answer is that the industry is relatively free of government interference.

Producers of goods and services in a free market know that if they provide quality products for reasonable prices, they will make money and that if they do not, they will go out of business. The economic bottom line is that if a producible good or service is in demand in a free market, profit-seeking businesspeople will endeavor to supply it at an affordable price.

Perhaps the most striking example of free-market productivity is the agriculture industry. The production of food is relatively unregulated in the United States. American farmers and ranchers own their own land and businesses; in many cases, although not all, they, not the government, decide what crops to plant, how much, what livestock to raise, how many, by what means to ship to market, and so forth. The result of a relatively free market of agricultural production is an enormous quantity and diversity of food-stuffs. We Americans often take for granted a visit to a US supermarket; but for one raised under socialism in which the government, not private farmers, controls production—in countries where the cupboards are bare and the food lines are long—a trip to an American grocery store is a wondrous experience. Free markets (and even relatively free ones) produce wealth. As the economic journalist Frédéric Bastiat noted about France's free market: "Paris gets fed." The Mises Institute website presents economics studies that speak to this topic.

On the other hand, government control creates poverty. As Milton Friedman, a Nobel Laureate in economics, once said: "If you put the federal government in charge of the Sahara Desert, in five years there would be a shortage of sand." This obviously is an exaggeration; nevertheless, Friedman's point is well-taken. The government is not a productive agency. This is why full socialism is always a hideous failure.

There is no exception to this in the area of education.

In a fully privatized free market of education, profit-seeking businesspeople would provide quality educational services at prices affordable to millions. And because they would have to meet consumer demand in order to thrive, they would provide a sweeping diversity of services matching actual student needs. For example, observing that many people value the full academic curriculum and want their children to learn the classic three Rs, entrepreneurial educators would provide such a service effectively and affordably.

Likewise, observing that many of these same people want their children later to advance to other academic subjects, educators would provide these services as well, because they could make money doing so.

The same is true of vocational training. Some families demand only the basics of academics and then want their children to branch out into one of many vocational fields—whether business, farming, baking, construction work, or countless other productive fields. In a free market, profit-seeking educators would supply such services as efficiently and inexpensively as possible—lest competitors provide a better value and put them out of business.

This truth also applies to the field of special education. Some individuals are gifted in specific ways—intellectually, musically, athletically—and require highly focused, advanced training. Others suffer from debilitating psychological or physiological ailments. Some are sadly afflicted with varying degrees of an intellectual disability. In a free market, where there is a demand for various forms of special education, profit-seeking businesspeople will compete to supply them.

All the evidence culled from the current state of education, from history, and from the logic of economics points without exception to a single conclusion: Private schools competing for students and profits in free (or freer) markets offer quality, affordable educational services to satisfy customer demand.

Converting the government schools into private schools isn't just a practical solution, however; it is a *moral* solution. A fully private school system would recognize and respect the rights of everyone involved. It would leave educators and customers fully free to produce and purchase educational products and services in accordance with their own needs and preferences.

Answering the Objections to Privatizing the School System

Before we turn to *how* the government school system could be privatized, let us address a couple of common objections to the goal of privatization. One is that some parents do not value their children's education enough to pay for it. To the extent that there are such parents, this is hardly a reason to violate the rights of all Americans and destroy the possibility of a good education for millions of other children. People who have children and do not care enough to educate them should be socially ostracized and, when appropriate, prosecuted for parental neglect. But they should not be held up as a reason to violate Americans' rights and keep American education in the sewer.

The fact is that the overwhelming preponderance of parents value their children's education *enormously* and, when free to choose how they would spend their money, would procure that value just as they do with food, clothing, shelter, and medical care. We have already discussed in this regard the increasing trend toward homeschooling in America. A growing number of parents, perhaps now in the millions, value their children's education so highly and are so dissatisfied with government schools that they have chosen to homeschool their children—despite the fact that they are generally still forced to finance the government schools they do not use. We have seen the excellent educational results of homeschooling.

If some parents choose not to provide their children with a proper education, that is their moral and legal right—and the children will, for a time, suffer the consequences of their parents' irrationality. But children are not mindless replicates of their parents; as they grow into adulthood they can and often do make fundamentally different choices. For example, children reared in one religion often choose another; the children of religious parents sometimes choose secularism; the offspring of bigoted parents often choose colorblind individualism; and the children of alcoholic or drug-addicted parents sometimes choose clean living. Human beings possess free will, and as numerous parents ruefully learn, their children frequently do not passively accept their families' values.

Even in today's government-thwarted education market, many centers of adult education prosper. A fully free market in education would enable educational entrepreneurs to expand this market immensely. Competition among teachers, tutors, and private schools providing both academic and vocational training for the adult market would increase; prices would drop; options would abound. In such a marketplace, the few children whose backward parents had neglected to educate them could seek education on their own in their early years of adulthood, then move on and live lives with greater wisdom and superior career opportunities.

Another objection to a fully privatized educational system is that if taxpayers were not coerced to finance government schools, some families would be unable to afford quality education. The first thing to note in addressing this is that the coercively funded and operated government schools are precisely what make it impossible for customers to receive quality education. Another important point is that with the government monolith slain, the property, income, and sales taxes that had been levied to sustain it could and should be repealed. With their tax burden substantially diminished, families would retain more of their income and be fully free to spend it on their children's education. Yet another point is that in a fully private market for education, competition among private schools, teachers, and tutors would increase dramatically. This inevitably would drive prices down, making education increasingly affordable.

As for those families that somehow in a free market for education still could not afford to pay for any education for their children, observe that even today many private schools offer scholarships to worthy students who cannot meet the tuition. In a fully free market for education, such scholarships would increase and abound. Private schools are highly competitive with one another, and they all seek to showcase the value and superiority of their product. Consequently, it is in their rational self-interest to attract students who will make them shine. Scholarships are a crucial means of doing so.

It is also worth noting that voluntary charity flourishes in America even when we are taxed at today's obscene rates. According to Giving USA's annual report on philanthropy, "Charitable giving in the United States exceeded $300 billion for the second year in a row in 2008," and "[e]ducation organizations received an estimated $40.94 billion, or 13 percent of the total."

In 2019, those totals rose to $449.64 billion and $64.11 billion, respectively. As long as the government does not prohibit educational charities, Americans will contribute to them. In short, in a fully private market for education, the few families unable to afford quality education would find no shortage of scholarships and/or charities available to assist them.

Objections to privatizing the government schools are simply false. So now let us turn to the question of how this privatization could be accomplished. There are, no doubt, several viable ways, but a straightforward one is simply auctioning off schools and their corresponding properties to the highest bidders. Either the sold schools would continue under private ownership, or the properties would be used for noneducational purposes. As noted above, if the schools were to become private, competition in a free market would ensure a drive toward improved education and decreased prices. If some of the properties were then deployed for noneducational purposes, the resultant increase in demand for education in that area would motivate profit-seeking educational entrepreneurs to meet the demand in other venues. Either way, the market would soon teem with private schools, teachers, and tutors competing to supply the educational service demanded by millions of families whose only earlier alternative was the abysmally bad government school system.

Such a transition would necessarily take some time, and the government would have to provide fair notice and appropriate grace periods to enable government-dependent families to adjust to the free market. For instance, the states could enact laws declaring that, effective immediately, the governments would begin auctioning off school properties, with transference of ownership to occur at the end of a five-year grace period. This would enable all teachers, tutors, and educational entrepreneurs to ramp up their businesses. And it would give all parents substantial time to assume full responsibility for the education of their children.

The enactment of such a policy would be followed by an explosion of private schools and tutoring services, some large scale, others small; some religious, some secular. *Every church and synagogue in the country would have a school*—as has so often been the case in the history of free countries. Some schools would be in private homes, some in multi-story buildings; some would be tiny community schools, some would be large educational corporations; some would be profit-driven, some not. The teeming diversity of schools and the high level of educational results would soon rival those of America in the centuries before the imposition of government schooling.

We who recognize the vital nature of education to the lives of individuals and to the health of a society should advocate the privatization of government-run schools and work toward the establishment of a fully private market in education.

The time to advocate this change is now.

CHAPTER SIXTEEN

What Schooling Could and Should Be Like

A friend of mine who teaches elementary school recently told me a true story. His students had read a children's version of *The Odyssey* in class. Homer's story, of course, features the attempt of Odysseus to return home to his loyal wife, Penelope, after ten years in the Trojan War. The story presents a riveting conflict: To get home, Odysseus must battle gods, monsters, witches, storms, and men. The kids loved it. One day, the father of a student had a tough time getting home after work. His commuter train broke down, the transit company transferred the passengers to buses, the bus got snarled in heavy traffic, and Dad was hours late getting home. The young student exclaimed, "It's like *The Odyssey*!"

An elementary school student who integrates the fiction he reads with real-life events shows his appreciation of great literature. What can we do to foster this attitude?

Philosophy of education is a complex field, and I certainly do not have all the answers. But in this chapter, I will make a number of recommendations that I believe will foster this attitude—and in so doing, greatly improve education in this country.

Elementary education is the foundation of learning. Because of this, it is the most important stage of education. In fact, preschool may be even more important. The earlier we start to effectively educate our children, the better it will be for them both in their learning and in their lives more broadly.

As I am a college professor, I am not an expert on elementary education. But for a variety of reasons, I know several important truths about it. First, I went through a government elementary school as a student in Brooklyn, and I remember a great deal about it. Second, I have forty years of teaching experience, mostly in colleges but also in high school. Third, I read to my daughter often when she was young, taught philosophy briefly at her Montessori school, and observed her cognitive development as she grew up. I have studied the field of education and thought about it long and hard.

Here is a modest proposal from someone who is an amateur in elementary teaching, but who knows a great deal about education in general.

Let us say that we have abolished the government school system and have repealed the property, income, and sometimes sales taxes that funded it. Families have more money to spend on schooling, and parental demand for education is strong. Most churches and synagogues establish schools. Thousands of tutors offer their services in every academic subject, both in person and online. An increasing number of parents homeschool their children—and join or form homeschool co-ops, in which parents take turns teaching the assembled kids the subjects each parent knows best. Countless small community schools are formed across the nation—and so forth.

Let's imagine that we set up a community school, hopefully small, but it could be larger. (Doing so does not require the abolition of government schools, of course, as many people have already done this.) We start at the elementary level. Let's say we start with ten students. I have a preference for small, cozy schools where each child gets a good deal of individual attention—but effective larger schools are certainly manageable. Here, in no particular order, are a number of points and policies that I recommend:

1. Starting Time

Start school later in the day, say at ten in the morning (or even later) rather than at eight or nine. The reason is that young children need more sleep than do older kids. As they get older, school can be started earlier (which also readies students to later on enter the work world). But if we are to hold high academic standards for young children, we must ensure they are properly rested.

2. Recreation and Rest

Make sure we have plenty of room and equipment for recreation. Children need to play. It is important for them. I intend to drive these kids hard academically, and they need rest and recreation—and lots of it—in between intense bouts of study. We need a yard and/or a gym where kids can

run, play ball, and can climb or swing on various appara-
tuses. We should also have a library stocked with fun books,
especially children's books, for the kids who want to relax
with a good story. If we start our school in the house of a
parent, we need one with a good-size yard and a rec room
with books, a few TVs, and headsets, so kids engaged in
different activities don't disturb each other. It is not that
expensive for parents to chip in and buy an outdoor jungle
gym; an assortment of balls, toys, and dolls; a bunch of kids'
books; an extra television or two, and a ping-pong table or
two. I want to stress this: Young children must have plenty
of playtime built into their school day.

3. Reading

The two most important subjects, by far, are reading and
writing. The ability to read well opens up the entire world
of knowledge to a child. A good reader, even if bored at
school, can still get an outstanding education by being an
autodidact and doing a great deal of reading. As an example,
although I hold a PhD in philosophy, I have learned much
more in my life by being an avid reader than I ever did in my
many years of college and graduate school. Indeed, some of
my closest friends never went to college but are very knowledgeable on a wide range of topics because, like me, they are
ferocious bookworms. Today, with so many of the world's
great books available for free online and/or just a few dollars
and a few days away via Amazon, it has never been so easy
for a bookworm to get a good education.

Continuing with this point, the first thing we need
to do is to show children that *books are fun*. So we stock a

wide array of inexpensive children's paperbacks in our rec room. They are there both for the children's free time and for their reading lessons. There are books about adventurous young boys and plucky young female detectives; true stories about heroes and heroines who overcame youthful obstacles to grow up and do great things; stories about ballplayers, scientists, explorers, writers, and daring mothers who escaped with their children from brutal dictatorships to freedom. There are also, as mentioned earlier, quirky stories about dogs that can fly, kittens who think the full moon is a bowl of milk, and bear cubs that have escaped from a zoo and, with the help of children, make it safely back into the mountains. Every day, in our reading lesson, a different child would pick out a book he or she prefers, and we, the teachers, would sit on the floor with the kids. They can stretch out and relax, and we will read a fun story to them. *The kids will learn that reading is fun!* They will want to learn to read, they will yearn to read independently, and they will desire to no longer need Mom or Dad or the teacher to read to them—but to be able to do it by themselves.

Once the children are super motivated, we would begin with training in systematic phonics. Reading class would be the longest and first class of the day, when the kids would be fresh. Every day, we would read fun books first and eventually add phonics training to class; within a few months, we would have a number of good students who, instead of the teacher, would read the fun stories aloud to the class. The kids would vie to be the chosen reader that day, and we would hold a friendly competition for the honor. The teachers would have an enormously empathic attitude toward the less advanced readers—never criticizing or ridiculing, always encouraging—and would make sure the advanced kids take the same good-natured attitude.

4. Goodwill in the Classroom

Indeed, empathy and kindness are essential attributes for a teacher to have—especially a teacher of young children. One sterling example was Marva Collins, one of America's greatest educators of the past fifty years. She combined a genuine love of the children with demanding academic standards; she challenged them, pushed them, and encouraged them. She hugged them; she showered them with physical affection, a positive message, and verbal support of their abilities; and she never lowered her standards. She expected and demanded great work of them, and in case after case, she received it. Her students excelled. I would make mandatory for every teacher or staff member at our school to view the outstanding film made about her life and career: *The Marva Collins Story*, starring Cicely Tyson and Morgan Freeman. It shows accurately how she took minority children often deemed uneducable by the public schools (from which she resigned) and via a combination of gentle love, tough love, and demanding academic work taught them to become superb students. Some young children learn to become excellent readers at a slower pace than others, and our teachers would support them with unslacking kindness and encouragement. The teachers' kindness toward all students would set an example for the kids, who would treat each other the same way. We would expect and demand benevolence from and for all. Our school would be a bastion of superior education and bottomless goodwill.

I have seen many times in my life, both as a student and as a teacher, that often a student can understand a difficult point when another student, rather than the teacher, puts it into his or her own words. *Students can be enormously helpful to their fellow students.* We would employ what has been long known as the monitor system, by which advanced students help younger students with their lessons. For example, those reading at a fourth-grade level or higher would help those at a first-grade level. Marva Collins was only one of many superb educators who employed this method to great effect. This type of helping system depends on a general attitude of goodwill in the classroom, which we would go to great lengths to foster.

5. The Importance of Writing

Writing is thinking on paper. Good writing is thinking well on paper. Reading and writing are the most important intellectual skills. Math and science are important disciplines, and we will teach plenty of each, but these fields, especially in their advanced forms, do not play a major role in most people's lives. For example, I have never used the math and sciences I studied in high school, and this is true of many people. These are fields that, to a great degree, can be left to the specialists. Later in the book you'll see the curriculum, including its math and science components, that I recommend.

But reading and writing cannot be left to the experts. As already noted, proficient reading opens up the entire world of knowledge to a human being. Writing effectively—including for people who do not aspire to be professional writers—involves organizing thoughts into coherent arguments; it requires creating a logical structure, offering evidence in support of a conclusion, and reasoning with clarity and precision. *Writing is reasoning.* All human beings, regardless of profession or interests, need to reason proficiently in order to lead a fulfilled life.

Some examples: A manager writes a project report at his job for a company manufacturing machine parts. An incensed homeowner writes a letter to the editor of her local newspaper about the new zoning restrictions imposed in her community. A young man sends an impassioned email to the woman he loves, expressing his deepest feelings; and she pours out her heart in an equally impassioned letter in return. Someone makes an important point on social media—and does it succinctly and effectively, displaying sharp thinking in few words. A customer writes a business letter to a long-patronized company to complain about the decline of a product or praise the firm's outstanding service. A scientist or mathematician wants to write up a new discovery so that the public may understand it. An entrepreneur seeks funding for a new venture and must compose a business plan to convince investors. A young student applies for a grant to attend a good school and must write a short essay explaining personal merits. And the beat goes on. Sharp thinking leads to sharp writing. Sharp writing is a consequence of sharp thinking. *Writing is not primarily a communicating skill. It is, first and foremost, a thinking skill.*

This would be the first and longest class of the day. Its fancy name is language arts. I think we should call it, more simply, reading and writing.

6. Schedule

Here is a proposed schedule for the school day.

- Ten to eleven a.m.: Reading and writing

- Eleven to eleven-thirty a.m.: Free time and play

- Eleven-thirty a.m. to twelve fifteen p.m.: Arithmetic, and more advanced math as the students progress

- Twelve fifteen to one fifteen p.m.: Lunch and play

- One fifteen to two p.m.: History—not social studies—including plenty of American history

- Two to two thirty p.m.: Free time and play

- Two thirty to three fifteen p.m.: Science

- Three fifteen p.m.: The school day ends.

7. Homework

There would be homework only in reading and writing. The children would have most of the rest of the day to themselves to do as they or their parents wish. We would work hard during class time and would not waste a second. The children would be rested and enjoy recreation. They would be motivated by the realization that afterschool hours belong to them. We would therefore be in a good position to push them hard in the important academic subjects—and we would. It does not take massive amounts of work for motivated students to learn basic academic concepts. What it takes is concentrated effort in delimited chunks of time. Some people think that a solid education in cognitive basics requires massive amounts of study. It does not. *It requires focused study in relatively short bursts.*

By midway through first grade, the students would be competent readers, and most of them would be superb, reading well above grade level. Learning to read is not the tortuous process that American schools have made it into. Reading is as natural to a healthy child as is running or riding a bike. Teaching reading effectively is simply a matter of showing children that books are fun—and then employing systematic phonics as the sole method to teach it.

By midway through first grade and continuing for the rest of their schooling, they would have literature homework. We would begin with outstanding children's books such as *The Secret Garden* and many by contemporary authors. The children would have a month to read each book. So, for example, on March 12, the teacher would issue an assignment: You must have *The Secret Garden* completed by April

12. Then from mid-April to mid-May, the class would discuss the book in depth, analyzing the characters, plot, theme, and writing. The children would be encouraged to speak about their impressions of the book, but the teacher would make sure that interpretations are backed by evidence from the story, and make clear that it is not the case that all interpretations are equal. *The events of a story are the facts of that universe.* It is with those events that the teacher would start the analysis of the book—just as scientists begin with observed facts as a means of forming theories about nature. Theories in literature, just as in science, must be grounded in facts—and must logically explain the facts.

From the first grade on, in literature and other subjects, the children would learn to reason.

8. Writing Instruction

Nearing the end of first grade, the students would be accomplished readers. And before the end of this grade, we would begin their writing instruction. We would start with the books we have read and discussed in depth. The students would write in class a paragraph or two about the book we have most recently studied. It is too soon to expect students to write complete essays, but here we would lay a foundation for future superlative writers. In the early grades, the teacher would assign a topic. As the kids become increasingly advanced readers and writers, the teacher would recommend they choose their own topic, although still assigning one for those who are uncomfortable doing so. But the teacher would make an important point: By third grade, after a year-plus of writing, the students would choose their own topic about a book. (It would be great if the alphabet was taught in K or pre-K. But even if it is not, we will teach it to kids in a matter of weeks in 1st grade.)

Even in college classes, some students are shy about taking such responsibility. The elementary teacher must be understanding and sensitive toward these children, must be enormously supportive and encouraging, and must hold the kids' hands through the process, but must be gently adamant that in time and with practice, the children would become independent regarding choosing writing topics—just as they learned to ride a bike without training wheels or a parents' hand steadying the bike. The teacher would grade these short works and spend time with each student individually, teaching how to improve his or her writing in numerous ways. Individualized work in the all-important field of writing is the greatest advantage of having small class sizes.

Also, from day one the teacher would be on the lookout for those kids so independent that they need to do things their own way; the teacher would encourage and nurture this trait, including by having these kids choose their own topic on their very first writing assignment. Independence is an enormously valuable characteristic; human society is moved forward by individuals who think outside the box, who do not conform to social norms, and who innovate new ideas, theories, and methods in any one of hundreds of fields. Just as important, self-directed children flourish in their own lives only when their capacity to function independently is encouraged—and as free-thinking adults, only when their right to do so is respected.

By third grade, the children would be ready to graduate from paragraphs to short essays. As already noted, the sole homework would be in reading and writing class. After a week of intense discussion, the teacher would assign a paper to be written at home, on a theme of each child's choosing, with a minimum length of five hundred words but with no maximum. Those kids excited about a specific book would be encouraged to write on it at greater length if they choose. When the assignments are handed in, the teacher would grade them carefully, discuss general writing techniques with the whole class, and engage in one-on-one discussion with each writer regarding his or her essay. Again, having small class sizes enables individual attention. But if the parents or teacher(s) or other people who run the school want it to grow, they would hire several qualified teachers. In some subjects, having larger numbers of students can work effectively. But the reading and writing class must have a small number of students. I cannot repeat this often enough: The teacher must give each student a great deal of individual attention in writing.

9. Reading List

What would be a proper reading list to develop reading comprehension and to encourage an appreciation of great literature? Earlier, we discussed Lisa VanDamme, who does a superb job educating students at VanDamme Academy in California. She mentions a number of excellent children's books that we could deploy in the early grades, including *Anne of Green Gables, The Secret Garden, An Indian in the Cupboard, The Witch of Blackbird Pond,* and *From the*

Mixed-Up Files of Mrs. Basil E. Frankweiler. The good news is that a number of authors have written excellent books for children and young adults; parents and teachers can decide which specific books they consider best for their kids. More to come regarding reading lists in the next chapter.

The Study of Heroes

We must include abundant heroes and heroines in our reading selections. One of the books I've written is titled *Heroes, Legends, Champions: Why Heroism Matters*. This is a philosophic book for adults, not for children. But why does heroism matter? For two reasons: One is that heroes perform life-promoting deeds, often against powerful obstacles and/or antagonism. Think of George Washington fighting with his ragtag army for freedom against the world's mightiest empire. Think of the opposition confronted by William Wilberforce as he sought to convince the British to become the first nation in history to abolish the slave trade and then to abolish slavery altogether. According to BrainyQuote: "Difficulties," said the great Antarctic explorer Ernest Shackleton, "are just things to overcome."

So heroes overcome powerful opposition to advance human life in any number of ways. The second reason heroism matters is that the sight of heroes facing daunting odds with calm courage, persevering in pursuit of life-promoting goals, and often triumphing over all impediments, is inspirational. It encourages us to be the best version of ourselves. Witnessing mighty heroes overcoming powerful opposition to attain life-giving goals fosters in us an attitude of respect for what our achievements might be if we confront the obstacles in our path with the determination and courage of a towering hero.

To contemplate a hero's life and achievements shows us the human potential. An attitude of honest hero worship is an enormously productive state of mind. All of us should allow ourselves to be inspired by heroes to improve ourselves—whether in terms of our education, character, relationship with other human beings, physical fitness, or one of a thousand other characteristics. A healthy hero worship is noble and life-improving. Above all, children should learn to cultivate such an attitude. It will serve them well as they struggle with obstacles in their lives.

The children in our school would read many books featuring heroes and heroines, and this would continue at least through twelfth grade—and hopefully, for the rest of their lives. The heroes would be of either gender; of any and all races, tribes, or nationalities; of any age; and from different eras; and they should courageously pursue important life-sustaining goals. For example, we could read of three musketeers who fight to defend France from dangerous villains. In a more advanced grade, we could read the story of a mighty Greek hero who fights monsters, gods, and men to return home from the wars to his beloved wife. And so on. And in history, of course, we will study the achievements of many great real-life heroes, whose stories can be integrated with the tales of fictional heroes. These might include Joan of Arc, the thirteen-year-old peasant girl who led the French armies to victory over the British— or perhaps George Washington Carver, who was born in

slavery, lost his mother, battled sickness and racism, overcame all obstacles, and became one of the great agricultural
scientists of history. Inspiring hero stories, both fictional
and true, are endless.

There are still other reasons that students should
read hero stories. One is that the sight of mighty heroes
confronting daunting obstacles and opposition in the
quest to accomplish important goals generates the essence
of great literature—conflict. The reader wants to find out
what happens—who wins the struggle? There is suspense,
and the reader gets caught up in the story—children learn
that reading is fun. Another is that children learn important
virtues from hero stories. They learn that courage is
important to achieve our goals in life; that the good is that
which advances human life in some way, shape, or form;
and that the good can triumph.

10.   Math

My final recommendation is about math. Many people
suffer from math anxiety and dread math tests. I was always
a mediocre math student at best; at worst, a failing one.
Algebra, in particular, never made sense to me, and I struggled with it. In part, the reason may be that I, and many
others, have little interest in or aptitude for the subject. But
I wonder if poor teaching contributes to the problem that
many of us have with it. I am no expert on teaching math.
But as a philosopher, I have an idea about it.

I will start with a true story. Years after I struggled
with math in high school, I studied philosophy in graduate school. In one course, we studied Aristotle's *Physics*.

We know today that Aristotle (384–322 BC) made many errors in this field. But he also made a number of important points. One that was enormously suggestive to me was his comment to the effect that mathematics studies the quantitative aspect of objects. This claim is succinct, insightful and, I think, both accurate and important. *The quantitative aspect of objects.* It hit me then that reference to objects was often missing from my earlier math classes; that is, there had been too little reference to observational reality, too few observable facts. The subject was taught in an overly abstract way. It occurred to me that math always should be taught by referencing observable objects—apples, let's say, or pennies, dollars, or blueberry muffins. To put it simply, math raises questions: How many dollars? How much of a muffin? How fast does the train go? *Math measures the quantitative aspect of things in our world.* And this is how it must be taught.

This is easily done in basic arithmetic. For example, if someone has three apples and is able to multiply that number by three, how many apples will the person have? This simply means that the person now has three groups, each with three apples. It is easy then to count the apples and come to the conclusion of nine total.

Take fractions as a second, more complex example. We divide an apple, let us say, into four equal parts; then we divide one of those four parts into two equal parts, and keep one of them. How much of the apple do we then have? It is easy to think, well, if we divided all four parts into two equal parts, there would then be eight parts to the apple. We have one of those parts, and one out of eight equals one-eighth of an apple.

As I said, algebra especially boggled me, for it deals with variables that could stand for a wide range of values. For example, take the simple equation 3a x 3 = 9a. What does the variable "a" stand for? *It could stand for any value, but it must stand for one.* This principle is important. Let's make sure we always translate variables into concrete values. So here is an equation: 3a x 3a -7 +4b + 12 = ? We give the equation first. But math studies the quantitative aspect of things in our world, right? So before we attempt to work out the equation, on the understanding that variables can stand for any value but must stand for some value, let's plug in some values for the variables.

I always loved sports, so I will make up a story that helps us visualize what the equation is talking about. We run a gym, let's say, and "a" stands for tennis balls and "b" for volleyballs. OK, fine, that's a good start. But I still want to know, when we subtract 7 and add 12, what are we subtracting and adding? Let's say those numbers refer to an amount of basketballs. So what is the equation talking about? Let's break it down: 3 tennis balls x 3 tennis balls = 9 tennis balls squared. This equals 81 tennis balls. We also have four volleyballs. We subtract 7 basketballs from our total of them and add 12, so we have 5 more basketballs than we had when we started. So the solution is: 81 tennis balls + 4 volleyballs + 5 basketballs additional to whatever was our previous amount of them. For me, as a weak math student, this helps my understanding, because it ties the problem to observed facts.

To repeat, I am a total amateur in math and in teaching it. My recommendations here might be simple-minded and/

or unworkable in some cases. Further, I showed these recommendations to a number of math experts and none agreed with me. But I strongly suspect that the more we tie math to concretes, observable objects and to the activities of and relationships between these objects, the easier we will make it for students of all ages to understand the subject. I suspect that my very weakness in this area gives me insight into the methods necessary to help other weak math students as well.

This is a point similar to one I made earlier, that a good teacher should start a discussion with examples and extract abstract ideas, concepts, or principles from the examples. This keeps the discussion tied to facts, to the real world— the discussion is at "sea level," as I like to say, rather than up in the clouds somewhere. This is the same reason that a good teacher should tell vivid stories to illustrate a complex theme. It is much easier to understand an idea when we have a real-world example or two. I believe this is as true in math as it is in any other field.

In the next chapter, we'll discuss curricula and priority— that is, the subjects to be taught and the order in which material within those subjects should be presented.

CHAPTER SEVENTEEN
Curricula and the Order of Presentation

Here is a thought experiment. Let us say we have a class of exceptionally bright seven-year-olds, some of whom will go on to get advanced degrees in mathematics years in the future. I tell my math colleagues, "Let's give these kids a head start. Let's teach them calculus." The math teachers look at me aghast. "Dr. Bernstein," they say. "These kids are advanced in arithmetic, no doubt. But they've never studied either algebra or trigonometry. They're not prepared for calculus." I wave my hand. "Bah!" I say in disgust. "They're smart kids. Let's teach 'em calculus."

Now, my idea is crazy—and the math teachers are right. There is a logical hierarchy of subject matter, an order in which material should be taught. Kids should read children's books before Shakespeare, learn about planetary orbits and gravity before Einstein's theory of relativity, learn a great deal of history and literature before tackling the abstract problems of philosophy, and so forth. So there are two questions: 1. What subject matter is necessary for a solid education? 2. In what order should this subject matter be presented?

Preschool and elementary education is the foundation of all learning. Let's focus on the early years, because if we get it right here, we will accomplish three things: 1. We will give children a powerful boost into the world of knowledge. 2. We will teach children the basic thinking skills of reading, writing, and math. 3. We will nurture in them a love of learning. This is an invaluable foundation for all future learning.

As noted, philosophy of education is an enormously controversial field, and I claim no expertise in it. Further, my abundant teaching experience is in higher education, not in the all-important early years. Nevertheless, two points are clear: 1. Current US schooling is a disaster. 2. Young children need to be trained in systematic phonics, to learn a wealth of facts, and to have a rigorous academic education.

I do not provide here a comprehensive plan of education, even for the early grades. Rather, I offer a series of suggestions that can substantially enhance a child's early education. I have studied excellent sources. One is *The Well-Trained Mind*, by Susan Wise Bauer and her mother, Jessica Wise. I strongly recommend it, especially for homeschoolers but additionally for all who are serious about significantly improving education in America. (I think of these two women as "the Wise Girls.")

One excellent point from this source is: "[Y]our number one goal should be to have your child reading fluently when [he or] she starts first-grade work." As mentioned earlier, not all parents can homeschool full-time. But, by using the methods already discussed, most parents can teach their children to read effectively before they start school. This type of part-time homeschooling is enormously. valuable. And as the authors point out in the same book, "Here is the good news: Reading is easy. We'll repeat that: Reading is easy. One more time: Reading is easy."

Some kids who are trained via phonics and get lots of support at home still struggle to read. I'm not sure if there are learning disabilities involved and/or other problems. But this much is sure: The overwhelming majority of children who are motivated to read by learning that books are fun and who are then taught to read via systematic phonics, learn early on to read effectively. Conversely, the majority of children who struggle to read suffer from one or both of the two following problems: Either they were not shown how enjoyable books are, and/or they were not taught to read by the use of phonics.

Another point made by Jessica Wise and Susan Wise Bauer is that "afterschooling" a child is often very effective. This is a process in which parents work with their children individually in the evening, on weekends, on holidays, and during summer vacation to repair damage done in the public schools or to enrich their classroom education. Today, parents should know how bad the schools are. If they feel a deficiency in their own skills, remember: The knowledge necessary to give young children a strong foundation in education is not that extensive, and many good books on elementary math, history, and so forth are available inexpensively through Amazon or free from the local library. Parents easily can obtain and read these books and use the information to teach their children.

Here is another true story. A friend of mine dated a young woman whose father was a successful banker. His daughter was very bright, and he wanted her to follow him into the field of finance. But she loved the hard sciences, not economics, and she went on to gain a PhD in chemistry. Her dad purchased a number of chemistry books and read them, so he could communicate with his daughter regarding her values. This is good parenting. Parents can act similarly on behalf of their young children. They can buy and read simple books on whatever subject and therefore be prepared to afterschool their young children effectively. For example, Mom might focus on science and math and Dad on literature and history—or vice versa, or tackle any combination of the subjects.

Here is another excellent point from the Wise Girls. Jessica Wise homeschooled her daughter, Susan. She writes in *The Well-Trained Mind*: "To begin with, I filled her head with facts when she was small." Remember Professor E.D. Hirsch and his discussions with professional educators who claimed that factual knowledge was useless? The Wise Girls agree with Hirsch. Presumably, Jessica taught her young daughter that the earth (and the other planets) revolves around the sun and does so in 365 days, constituting a terrestrial year. The moon revolves around the earth. America's War of Independence against Great Britain began in April 1775 with the "shot heard round the world," fired by the American Minutemen against British troops in Concord and Lexington, Massachusetts. George Washington was the first US president. The Thirteenth Amendment ending slavery in America was passed in 1865. The Himalayan

Mountains are in Asia, the Alps in Europe, the Rockies in North America, and the Andes in South America. And so forth. The Wise Girls are correct: Facts are the building blocks of knowledge—and many young children are eager to learn. Also, Jessica showed Susan that books are fun and taught her to read early. Someone who reads for fun is likely to find a great deal of useful information in books.

Teaching History

I love Jessica Wise's approach to teaching history. It is not original to the Wise Girls; it is a classical approach, and the Wise Girls strongly recommend it. Let me break the approach into parts. There are three important points regarding the teaching of history.

1. **Teach history in three repetitions of a four-period cycle**. Each cycle goes over the same time periods but in rising levels of complexity. So, for example, in grades one, five, and nine, the kids study ancient history, roughly from 5000 B.C. to 400 A.D. In grades two, six, and ten, they study medieval and early-Renaissance history, roughly the years of A.D. 400 to A.D. 1600.

   In grades three, seven, and eleven, the kids study late-Renaissance and early-modern history, roughly from 1600 to 1850. In grades four, eight, and twelve, the kids study modern history, from roughly 1850 to the present. The Wise Girls write in the same book: "The child studies these four time periods at varying levels—simple for grades 1 through 4, more difficult in grades 5 through 8 (when the student begins to read original sources), and taking an even more complex approach in grades 9 through 12, when the student works through these time periods using original sources (from Homer to Hitler)."

2. **Integrating History and Literature**: The teachers integrate other subjects into the historical periods studied. So when the kids study ancient history, their literature classes initially will involve reading Greek and Roman mythology, Chinese and Japanese fairy tales, and the myths of other cultures. As they cycle back to the ancient period at a more advanced level, their literature readings will include *The Iliad*, *The Odyssey*, *The Aeneid*, and early medieval writings. During the last cycle through of ancient history, the students will read the works of Plato, Aristotle, Herodotus, and so forth in their literature course.

The same approach to literature is taken throughout the children's schooling; the literature of a period is integrated into the study of its historic events. So when studying medieval and Renaissance history, the students will read *Beowulf* and works by Dante, Chaucer, and Shakespeare. When reviewing eighteenth- and nineteenth-century history, they will start with Jonathan Swift's *Gulliver's Travels*, conclude with Charles Dickens, and presumably read works by the likes of Voltaire, Benjamin Franklin, and Jane Austen in between.

3. **Integrating History and Science**: Science is united with the history program as well. In *The Well-Trained Mind*, the Wise Girls write: "The sciences are studied in a four-year pattern that roughly corresponds to the periods of scientific discovery: biology, classification, and the human body (subjects known to the ancients); earth science and basic astronomy (which flowered during the early Renaissance); chemistry (which came into its own during the early Modern period); and basic physics and computer science (very modern subjects)."

Consider the virtues of this approach. "Those who fail to learn from history are condemned to repeat it," said Winston Churchill in a paraphrase of a famous remark by philosopher George Santayana. For example, let us say we seek to understand the 2021 rise of the Taliban to power in Afghanistan. We would first need to understand who the Taliban are; that they were born out of the 1980s religious fighters that received massive American aid in their struggle against Soviet invasion. In order to understand US involvement in this conflict, we would need to understand the Cold War. But the Cold War emerged as a result of World War II, which was caused by the rise of totalitarianism in Russia, Italy, and Germany, brutal dictatorships that cannot be understood unless we comprehend the blood bath and results of World War I, which was caused by.... And the beat goes on. Human society is organic. Every major event ripples through the decades, continuing to engender consequences even centuries in the future. *Where the world is in any moment in time is a direct function of where it has come from in the past.* The approach to history advocated by the Wise Girls provides students completing the program with a profound understanding of history that will contribute to an equally profound understanding of current events. But when this type of historical approach is integrated with the literature and science of each period, the result is a superlative education *achieved by the twelfth grade.*

Teaching Causation in History

I will add my own thoughts on teaching academic subjects. Regarding history, we must focus on essentials—the politics, the kings and emperors, their deeds and misdeeds, and the wars, religion, art, literature, and philosophy of the era. Eliminate all minutiae. For example, we do not need to know what type of fish a certain people favored, how they prepared it, and what they wore. *We must show the cause-and-effect relationships in history.* As one example, Alexander the Great conquered the Middle East, including ancient Judea; the rational, secular culture of the Greeks clashed with Orthodox Judaism. This led to the uprising of the Maccabees and the triumph of Orthodox Jews over Hellenized Jews (those committed to Greek culture). In time, Rome conquered Greece and established a far-flung empire, including subjugating Judea. But Greek culture dominated Roman thinking. The Jews rose up again in two bloody rebellions against the largely secular Roman rule. The Romans suppressed these insurrections brutally; in one, they destroyed the Second Temple in Jerusalem; after the other, they exiled the Jews from their ancient homeland, creating a diaspora whose effects rippled for centuries. This ripple effect included the Zionist movement's reestablishment of the Jewish state in its ancient land, in territory that had been conquered and held for centuries by Muslims, many of whom regarded Islam as the one true faith and some of whom were fiercely hostile to the establishment of a Jewish state on "their" land. We know the endless cycle of violence that ensued. Indeed, for those who know history, the incessant violence was predictable.

What is the takeaway of this true story? Among others, that major historic events often lead to effects centuries, even millennia, into the future. This is what students must be taught in their history courses.

Teaching Literature

Regarding literature, I made an earlier point that cannot be repeated often enough: *The events of a literary work are the facts of the universe presented in that work.* Notice that scientists observe nature and identify, among other facts, that hot air rises, that cows have four distinct compartments to their stomachs, that water freezes at thirty-two degrees Fahrenheit, and so on. They then reason, theorize, and experiment, attempting to explain the causes of such phenomena. Their theories must logically—that is, without contradiction—explain the observed facts. If a theory clashes with observed facts, then it must be jettisoned, and the scientists must start over.

It is similar with literature. An interpretation of a story must be logically based in and congruent with the events of the story; if a literary theory clashes with the events of a story, it is wrong and must be discarded. *Not all literary interpretations are of equal value.* All interpretations should be welcomed and discussed seriously in class, without ridicule, just as all scientific theories should be welcomed and seriously discussed; but, in both fields—art and science—we seek the theory that most consistently and without contradiction explains the facts. In literature, there may be ambiguity, levels of meaning or contrasting meanings; but in such cases, we look for competing interpretations that (roughly) explain the events equally well, and discard those that do not. Then we scrutinize the two finalists to see if one has superior explanatory power. The facts of each world, fictional or real, are the final arbiter and highest court of appeal regarding the truth of any theory.

Teaching Science

Based on the above discussion, and more fundamentally on scientific method, it should be clear how science courses must proceed. They must emphasize observable facts, theory formation, and experimentation. Scientists observe data, form a theory to explain the data, and devise experiments to test the theory; the observed results of the experiment tend to corroborate or falsify the theory. If the factual results support the theory, other scientists seek to replicate it; if the observed results of the experiment consistently falsify the theory, scientists scrap the theory and seek to develop an alternative one. But observed facts are the touchstone of a theory's truth or falsity.

Aristotle observed long ago that man is a rational animal. Our reasoning faculty not only fundamentally distinguishes us from other animals, but we now understand that it is mankind's survival instrument. The novelist and philosopher Ayn Rand presents this point brilliantly in her great novel *Atlas Shrugged*. She shows that just as birds have wings to fly, lions have claws and fangs to tear apart their prey, antelopes have foot speed to outrun lions, and so forth, man has the intelligence to grow crops, cure diseases, build homes and cities, and achieve much more. But our intelligence must be nurtured; it must be taught. Above all, the purpose of education should be to teach our children to think. The essence of reasoning is to provide factual evidence to support a conclusion. This method should be deployed by every teacher, in every course, in every grade. *The students will thereby experience reasoning in action.* Then they can study it explicitly.

Teaching Logic

I recommend a yearlong course in the history of Western philosophy for twelfth graders, using a sophisticated college-level text: the first four volumes of W. T. Jones' *A History of Western Philosophy*. In that course, students would study the theories of the greatest philosophers of history, seeking answers to mankind's most pressing questions: What is human nature? What is the nature of the universe taken as a totality? What is the good? What is the good society? And, finally, how do we gain knowledge? Students would spend a good amount of time studying the Greeks, especially Aristotle, arguably the greatest philosopher of all. Among numerous other accomplishments, he founded the field of logic, which the students would take several weeks to study. They would learn the rules of proper reasoning, and the major errors of reasoning—the logical fallacies. They would analyze arguments regarding current, real-life issues, and ask such questions as: Is the evidence provided relevant to the conclusion? If so, is the evidence sufficient to establish the conclusion? Logic would be, in effect, a course within the larger philosophy course. By the end of twelfth grade, the students will have experienced reasoning in practice for twelve years and will have studied it in theory in the logic course. Reasoning will first have been shown to them and then theoretically explained to them. *This integration shows them how to be thinkers.*

For those who believe that such an approach is too intel-lectually demanding for many students, I recommend they watch or rewatch the superb 1988 film *Stand and Deliver*, based on the true story of how teacher Jaime Escalante helped transform a number of low-income, minority teenagers—whom the school's administrators had deemed unsuited for high-level subjects such as calculus—into outstanding math students. Also, as cited numerous times in this book, Marva Collins achieved similar superlative results working with minority kids often deemed ineducable by the public schools. A combination of tough love, tender love, superb teaching, and *very high academic expectations* can enable millions of students to gain an outstanding education.

The Order in Which Material Should be Taught

Regarding the question of what should be taught, the above discussion provides a number of solid answers. Now we must confront the next question: In what order should these subjects be presented? I have mentioned the educator Lisa VanDamme and her academy several times. She wrote an essay titled, "The Hierarchy of Knowledge" that was published in the Spring 2006 issue of *The Objective Standard*. In it, she provides a number of insights regarding hierarchy, or the proper order in which materials should be taught. In literature, for example, she recommends starting young children with great children's books such as *Anne of Green Gables*, *The Secret Garden*, and *An Indian in the Cupboard*. She writes in this essay: "Children's novels are written for children: They have plots that enthrall children, characters to which children can relate, and themes that children can understand." She is correct, of course. Relatable stories teach children the all-important lesson that *reading is fun*!

She recommends that around the fifth grade, children read great plays before jumping into great adult novels. The reason is that plays are simpler: They cannot explore the inner thoughts of their characters, they are limited in space and time period, and they must be sufficiently brief to be acted out on stage in a few hours. They therefore serve as an excellent transition between outstanding children's novels and the greatest novels (and other works) of adult literature. Some of the plays she recommends for these middle years of a child's education are *The Miracle Worker*, *An Enemy of the People*, *The Winslow Boy*, *Inherit the Wind*, *Twelve Angry Men*, and *Pygmalion*.

When kids enjoy and analyze shorter and relatively simpler works of outstanding literature, they are prepared, as they pass through puberty and then into high school, for the greatest of literary works: *Oedipus the King*, *Antigone*, *Macbeth*, *Hamlet*, *Paradise Lost*, *Cyrano de Bergerac*, *Pride and Prejudice*, *The Scarlet Letter*, *Moby Dick*, *A Tale of Two Cities*, *Huckleberry Finn*, *Crime and Punishment*, and many more.

VanDamme also provides valuable insights regarding the order in which scientific principles should be taught. She points out that to teach science in the right order, we must begin with simple observable facts and proceed to more complex theories. A proper approach to science teaching, she argues, is historical, because the simpler discoveries were necessarily made first. She teaches science primarily by experimentation. In the early grades, the kids learn the principles closest to the observational level; the experiments demonstrate the principles in action—so the kids see the principles for themselves. The experiments are simple, demonstrating friction and air pressure. Children taught in this way see the relevant principle; it is demonstrated by means of observation. This is science at "sea level," not up in the clouds somewhere.

Then VanDamme builds historically, using experiments to show essential scientific principles in the order in which they were discovered. She ties to observational reality the principles identified by great scientists such as Eratosthenes, Aristarchus, Copernicus, Kepler, and Galileo. This way, the students learn 1. the facts that support major scientific truths, and 2. the logical relationship between scientific truths, which are simpler and which are more complex, which logically come first and which depend on the others.

Only then does she get to Newton. His monumental identification of the laws of motion was based on these earlier discoveries and his own, which the students are now ready to understand. They have the historic context and the scientific foundations necessary to understand Newton's experiments, thought processes, and sweeping conclusions. Now they are ready to study Newton and see the truth of his conclusions, to "see it like a truck." And we can conclude that this is an excellent method by which to teach science.

I don't know a definitive theory of education. At this point in human development, I'm not sure that anybody does. But implementing a number of suggestions made in this book would lead to significant improvement in the state of American education. I want to point out to parents: At the very least, it will not take much to improve upon the dismal "education" provided today by America's public schools.

Summary

We have discussed a number of important points in this short book.

We have validated the widely recognized belief that American public schooling is generally terrible. We have also discussed a truth, surprising to some, that American education was not always poor. Indeed, prior to the imposition of government schools in the mid nineteenth century, American education was predominantly private and generally outstanding. I went on to relate the sad story of how (and by whose harmful influence) American education degenerated in the twentieth and twenty-first centuries until it reached today's sorry state. I also briefly told the story of heroic defenders of intellectual training and how their principles—especially those of Maria Montessori—point the way to a renaissance in American education. We also have discussed how the sorry state of teacher training mirrors that of academic education in the public schools. After all, if the schools teach little of academic subjects to the kids, how much of those subjects must teachers know?

We examined the power brokers in American schooling. The schools of education, the state departments of educa-

tion, the federal Department of Education, and local superintendents, principals, and school administrators form
what Arthur Bestor named the interlocking directorate.
It controls all aspects of American schooling, and it is, as
E.D. Hirsch calls it, an impregnable fortress, 100 percent
invulnerable to criticism or attempts at reform. Parents, said
former Virginia governor Terry McAuliffe in a perfect state-
ment of the fortress' invulnerability, should not tell public
schools what they can or cannot teach their children.

But we have seen that the exact opposite is true. *If
education is to be vastly improved in this country, parents—
and nobody else—must have 100 percent control over what is
and is not taught to their children.* We examined a number of
instances—in the past and present, overseas and at home—
in which parents have, at the very least, a great deal of
control over what and how content is taught. We have noted
the positive academic outcomes.

We have discussed a number of specific suggestions to
improve American education. And, finally, I have presented a
bold proposal to abolish government schools and completely
privatize American education. The educational benefits of
this would be immense.

The key takeaways from this book are that parents—not
the state—have the rightful power to educate their children,
and the time to act on this truth is now.

Bibliography

Bestor, Arthur, *Educational Wastelands: The Retreat from Learning in Our Public Schools*. Urbana, Ill.: University of Illinois Press, 1953.

Coulson, Andrew, *Market Education: The Unknown History*. New Brunswick, NJ: Transaction Publishers, 1999.

Collins, Marva and Tamarkin, Civia, *Marva Collins Way*. New York: Putnam, 1990.

Dewey, John, *The School and Society*. Chicago: University of Chicago Press, 1991.

Dewey, John, *Experience and Education*. New York: Collier Books, 1938.

Flesch, Rudolf, *Why Johnny Can't Read: And What You Can Do About It*. New York: Harper & Row, 1955.

Grabar, Mary, *Debunking Howard Zinn: Exposing the Fake History that Turned a Generation Against America*. Washington, D.C.: Henry Regnery, 2020.

Gross, Martin, *The Conspiracy of Ignorance: The Failure of American Public Schools*. New York: Harper Collins, 1999.

Hirsch, E.D., *The Schools We Need and Why We Don't Have Them*. New York: Random House, 1996.

Heard Kilpatrick, William, *The Montessori System Examined*, Boston: Houghton Mifflin, 1914.

Kronen, Laura, *Homeschool Happily*. Atlanta: Independently Published, 2020.

Montessori, Maria, *The Montessori Method*. Middletown, Del.: Create Space Independent Publishing Platform, 2014.

Peikoff, Leonard, "The American School: Why Johnny Can't Think" in Ayn Rand, *The Voice of Reason: Essays in Objectivist Thought*. New York: Penguin, 1990.

Peterson, Robert, "Education in Colonial America," in *Public Education and Indoctrination*. Irvington-on-Hudson, NY: The Foundation for Economic Education, 1993.

Ravitch, Diane, *Left Back: A Century of Failed School Reforms*. New York: Simon and Schuster, 2000.

Ravitch, Diane and Finn, Chester, *What Do Our 17-Year-Olds Know? A Report on the First National Assessment of History and Literature*. New York: Harper & Row, 1987.

Sowell, Thomas, *Inside American Education: The Decline, The Deception, The Dogmas*. New York: The Free Press, 1993.

Standing, E.M., *Maria Montessori: Her Life and Work*. New York: Plume, 1998.

Tooley, James, Really Good Schools: Global Lessons for High-Caliber, Low-Cost Education. Oakland, Cal.: The Independent Institute, 2021.

Wise Bauer, Susan and Wise, Jessica, *The Well-Trained Mind: A Guide to Classical Education at Home*. New York: W.W. Norton & Company, 2004.

Websites Referenced

A School website, https://a.school.

Atlas Academy website, https://atlas-academy.org.

Barkoukis, Leah, Townhall, "Shocking Data Out of Baltimore High School Shows How Many Kids Can Only Read at Elementary Level," February 3, 2022, https://townhall.com/tipsheet/leahbarkoukis/2022/02/03/baltimore-hs-reading-level-n2602779.

Barrington, Kate, "New Study Confirms That Private Schools Are No Better Than Public Schools," December 13, 2021, https://www.publicschoolreview.com/blog/new-study-confirms-that-private-schools-are-no-better-than-public-schools?cv=1.

Borders, Max, "#2—Because We're Running Out of Resources, Government Must Manage Them," April 22, 2014, https://fee.org/articles/2-because-were-running-out-of-resources-government-must-manage-them/#:~:text=Milton%20Friedman%20once%20said%2C%20%E2%80%9CIf%20you%20put%20the,very%20serious%20problem%20with%20government%20management%20of%20resources.

BrainyQuote; https://www.brainyquote.com/quotes/ernest_shackleton_179199.

Literacy Statistics, 2022, https://www.thinkimpact.com/literacy-statistics/.

Callahan, Gene, "What Is Economics? Why Study It?" June 18, 2002, https://mises.org/library/what-economics-why-study-it#:~:text=In%20the%20nineteenth%20century%2C%20French%20economist%20Fr%C3%A9d%C3%A9ric%20Bastiat,Economics%2C%20rather%2C%20must%20explain%20how%20it%20comes%20about.

Faulconer, Jeanne, "What Is a Homeschool Co-op?" https://www.Thehomeschoolmom.com/what-is-homeschool-co-op.

"Germany Is Desperate for Teachers," DW Made for Minds, August 27, 2018, https://www.dw.com/en/germany-is-desperate-for-teachers/a-45246978.

Hooked on Phonics website, https://hookedonphonics.com.

McDonald, Kerry, "Got Teacher Burnout? Launch a Microschool," *Forbes*, November 24, 2021, https://www.forbes.com/sites/kerrymcdonald/2021/11/24/got-teacher-burnout-launch-a-microschool/?sh=2725c4be116d.

"Establishing Your Microschool," Microschool Revolution website, https://www.microschoolrevolution.com/founder-article/establishing-your-microschool/.

Outschool website, https://outschool.com/#abl0engfl6.

Parents website, https://www.parents.com.

Prenda website, https://prenda.com.

Prothero, Arianna, "What Is a Microschool and Where Can You Find One?" January 2016, https://www.edweek.org/policy-politics/what-is-a-micro-school-and-where-can-you-find-one/2016/01.

Ray, Brian D. Ph.D., "Homeschooling: The Research," September 9, 2021, https://www.nheri.org/research-facts-on-homeschooling.

Snoyer, Manisha, "How I Started My Own School and You Can too," https://manisharoses.medium.com/how-i-started-my-own-school-and-you-can-too-9861cda90ee2.

Varsity Tutors website, https://www.varsitytutors.com.

"We Don't Need to Change Everything in Education, Just a Few Things," Brave Generation Academy, September 20, 2021, https://www.bravegenerationacademy.com/2021/09/22/we_dont_need_to_change_everything_in_education_just_a_few_easy_things.

"What Research Says About Parent Involvement," Responsive Classroom, 2022, https://www.responsiveclassroom.org/what-research-says-about-parent-involvement/.

Acknowledgments

Much of this book is based on two essays I published in *The Objective Standard*: "Heroes and Villains in American Education" and "The Educational Bonanza in Privatizing Government Schools." I would like to thank Craig Biddle, editor and publisher of that outstanding journal, for his permission to use this material—and both Craig Biddle and Jon Hersey for their superb editing of those essays.

Additionally, Paul and Gail Saunders provided helpful feedback on early drafts of the manuscript. Michael Gustafson—who, with his wife, Iara, founded and runs Atlas Academy in Dracut, Massachusetts—was a wealth of information. Melanie Hoffman, a homeschooling mom, graciously filled out a questionnaire regarding her successful experience teaching her own children.

I have many friends with whom I've spent many hours discussing American education—its failings and the solutions. They know who they are.

I am indebted to all of these individuals for their invaluable help in preparing this book.

About the Author

Vanessa Maxwell,
House of Maxwell
Photography

Andrew Bernstein holds a PhD in philosophy from the City University of New York. He has taught philosophy for many years in several New York–area colleges and universities. He went through the public school system K–12 in Brooklyn, NY, and has taught thousands of public high school graduates in his career. He has witnessed firsthand the decline of the American school system. He has been named "teacher of the year" at the State University of New York at Purchase and at Marymount College. He lectures across the country and around the world on a variety of topics related to education. He spent a year teaching at the American University of Bulgaria and witnessed the shocking truth that Bulgarian students very often mastered written English better than most American students.